DELAYS AHEAD: BE PREPARED TO STOP

When Silence is the Only Language God Speaks

Dr. Roberto Pérez

Cataloging-in-Publication Data is available.
ISBN 978-0-578-94928-4 (paperback);
ISBN 978-0-578-94963-5 (ebook)

Book design by Juan Espinoza Pérez,

R.J. Delays Ahead: Be Prepared to Stop. When Silence is the Only Language God Speaks

Acknowledgements

First, I must thank God for allowing me the privilege of serving Him. My life has been an incredible journey through many mountain and valley moments. God has been the designer of so many of those moments. Yes, there are those life experiences I hope I will never repeat, but if I had to live again, I would not change a thing. It is an unbelievable joy to serve God, my friends in the United States, and those on the mission field.

To my parents, thank you for investing in me. You allowed me to experience missions as a kid. You were intentional about connecting me with my natural inclinations. You prayed for me when I was trying to discover who I was as an individual.

To my wife, you are strong. You are beautiful. You are godly. And I love doing life with you.

To my kids, thank you for being such awesome kids. You are both incredible women of God. I want the world to know I am proud of the two of you. God gave me two special gifts when you were born.

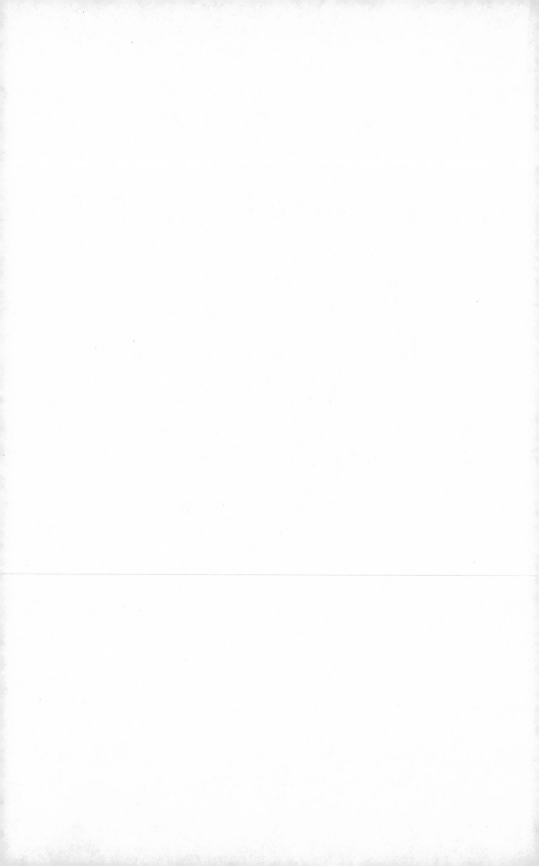

CONTENTS

INTRODUCTION

...the most hopeful thing any of us can say about spiritual transformation: I cannot transform myself, or anyone else for that matter. What I can do is create the conditions in which spiritual transformation can take place, by developing and maintaining a rhythm of spiritual practices that keep me open and available to God.[1]

For the past year, I've been visiting many churches and different individuals in my role as a missionary communicator. I've noted that you tend to do one of two things. Either you rely on yourself as a communicator on repeat, or you seek God to use you daily, knowing that the message inside of you is God-inspired, God-designed, and God-authored for each audience. I like to think that I often choose the latter, but if I were honest with myself as a communicator, I'd admit that this is not always the case. You see, life tends to be so much easier on repeat. We can snooze the alarm, spend more time in front of the TV, relax through our hobbies, and the intentionality needed to hear God slowly dissipates. Most likely, we'll never make a single concerted decision toward living life on repeat, but yes, it happens through the everyday rhythms of life. But what happens when life consistently intersects with the challenge of using intentionality for hearing God? All too often, we gradually allow life stressors to dictate to us that we choose the road of least resistance. When we do, we allow ourselves to fall into the surprising easiness of relying on ourselves while unintentionally forgoing the listening that connects us to God's still, small voice.

Our family has lived in Latin America for many years. We

spent our first missionary assignment in Chile, living at the base of the majestic mountains surrounding Santiago, the capital city. A few years later, we were transferred to San Jose, Costa Rica, where we lived in a valley full of some of the most amazing views. These views were so spectacular that visitors to our country were often mesmerized by their beauty. In fact, so were we! We could sit outside of our back yard in Chile and see the snow-capped mountains that surrounded us almost all year round. Driving through Costa Rica allowed us to see active volcanos regularly. The lush green jungles enveloped me quite often as I drove out to meet with my friends on the Eastern coast of Limon. I cherish those unforgettable experiences as a missionary—experiences I wouldn't have had if I had lived my entire life in the United States. Who gets to go to work with a machete, ride in canoes, cross raging white water rapids as the rain causes deadly water risings, and witness mudslides that bring traffic to a halt? During the honeymoon stage, when everything is new and beautiful in life overseas, God's amazing creations often leave you awestruck.

But something happens, and the new becomes ordinary.

The majestic becomes your everyday experience and may lead to feelings of frustration. When the volcano in Turrialba erupts for days on end, and volcanic ash covers your house inside and out, your feelings of amazement start changing. Driving through some of the deadliest roads (Cerro de la Muerte, Braulio Carrillo), the build-up of traffic and slow-moving vehicles begin to take their toll on you. Your frustration is magnified when the fogged-over road with zero visibility stretches on for long periods. When a three-mile drive turns into a daily ninety-minute commute full of torrential downpours, something begins to change in you—you begin to lose sight of the God-factor. The beauty, the splendor, the fantastic touch of God's handiwork that once delighted you slowly fades into the background until one day it's gone. The worst thing is you don't even realize it. The God-awe that once thrilled you is now replaced by the ordinary, the mundane.

To hear God takes incredible amounts of patience. We can't rush God; we can't force God to speak.

While many have tried to write books, conduct seminars, and teach a formula to hear from God, there's no one-size-fits-all methodology to achieve that purpose. And therein lies the problem!

God will never allow His guiding voice to be reduced to a human-concocted methodology or manufactured prescription. Principles are essential and biblical truths are priceless, but when we look at Scripture in its totality, we see God has chosen many ways to speak to people. We can't bottle up a solution that will work for everyone; I doubt it can be done at all—let alone "simply." It was never God's intention for people to understand His divine thinking, acting, or being completely. Isaiah 55:8 tells us that "...my thoughts are not your thoughts, neither are your ways my ways." And just when we think we have God all figured out, He does something so out of the ordinary, something so unexpected, that we're forced to stay steady in prayer, Bible study, and a state of keeping the faith. Sometimes, it causes us to respond in the same way as Job's wife when she said, "Do you still hold fast your integrity? Curse God and die" (Job 2:9).

Recently I came across a quote by Winston Churchill that indirectly speaks to this challenge. He said:

> Every prophet has to come from civilization, but every prophet has to go into the wilderness. He must have a strong impression of a complex society and all that it has to give, and then he must serve periods of isolation and meditation. This is the process by which psychic dynamite is made.[2]

Churchill undoubtedly had his hardships in life, but his words bring some perspective to our walk with God. He believed the prophet was a powerful voice for society, but unless the prophet walked through what he called the wilderness experience, that voice would never develop its full potential. It was his opinion that the wilderness experience gave the "dynamite flare" to the prophet. This dynamite flare is God's intention for the Christian life.

Can you be a prophet, communicator, minister, or Christ-follower if you rely on yourself? I'd say the answer is yes, but I'd also argue that you miss out on the single most influential component that gives you that "dynamite edge." I call it "the God-awe."

This book doesn't claim to be a self-help manual describing a program to overcome life obstacles. *Delays Ahead: Be Prepared to Stop* is the story of one missionary family's journey of experiencing the multifaceted inaudible guiding voice of God. My prayer is for you to understand that there's no one way to describe God's voice. Scriptures show us a God of diversity. And yes, I think that this is intentional on God's part. In your own way and based on your experiences, I hope you'll learn to hear the voice of the Holy Spirit. I pray that you'll discover that whether you're dealing with the mundane moments, the gradual absence of the God-awe, the unmistakable silence of the God's voice, God will always be writing your story with His mark of penmanship.

There will be days when you deal with life's mundane moments or feel the gradual absence of the God-awe. When you can't hear the God-voice or wonder why He seems to have disappeared or doesn't answer, He is still present. When you walk with Jesus, God is always writing your story.

IN THE BEGINNING

May we never lose our wonder – Bethel Music

Families are something that none of us will ever choose! If you have ever heard me preach during our fundraising cycles, you'll realize that I almost always begin by showing a picture of my family. I then say, "What I love about that picture is that it creates a connection point that resonates with every one of us, whether man, woman, boy or girl, and that connection point is our story." I can guarantee that behind every picture is a story: a story of what we were doing, where we were, or maybe even the family arguments that took place while the photographer took the picture, but in the end, we were all smiling.

However, if we dig a little deeper, that picture may represent a bigger story. Maybe the photographer took it at a time when things were hard. That picture might remind us of people who are no longer with us, our decisions, or some other event in life. We might surround ourselves with family pictures to help us connect with those people emotionally because somehow, we've isolated ourselves from them. Maybe we never enjoyed the growing up of our children, the birth of grandchildren, or the joys we experience living in relationship. Our family has lived abroad for the entirety of our kids' lives. We made sure there were always pictures to remind our kids of their family so they could identify each one of their aunts and uncles. Our absence from our extended family wasn't our choice. We were absent from our family because God had a mission for us. All four of us! I say that because the missionaries weren't just Bob and Michele. They were Bob, Michele, Priscilla, and Isabella.

My kids didn't get to choose where they'd grow up, and neither did I. They never asked to grow up in another culture with a language that wasn't theirs, nor did they ask to be ripped away from their friends and family every few years. As a parent, I still remember how I wrestled with my feelings the first time my mom visited us in Santiago, Chile.

We had not seen her for nearly a year. We were fresh off a plane moving from Costa Rica after our time at the language school had ended. Arriving in Chile, we immediately had to start with our foreign ministry. A national general assembly was taking place within the Assemblies of God at the time. At this event, we were to be introduced to all of our denomination's pastors; there would be many daily meetings and meals. This environment wasn't great for our kids because they were so young. Our missionary mentor arranged for them to stay at home with a non-English speaking nanny. My kids were terrified, and so were their mom and dad. A new country, a different language, and we were away from our kids! *¡Que terror* (Talk about scary)! When I told my mom, she said, "I'm coming to Chile." And she did. The kids almost had a heart attack when they saw her.

To be honest, before I got to my house, I took her to a slum apartment complex and said, "Welcome home, Mom. We live here." The woman almost died. She tried to smile and suck it up, but she was speechless until I said, "No worries, I'm just kidding." We laughed all the way to the temporary apartment where we lived.

When the day came for Mom to go home, we all cried as she entered the airport. Leaving the parking lot, I had to pull over because I was losing it emotionally. My kids were crying hysterically. I couldn't believe I was the reason for those tears. I came to Chile because I had heard God, not them. I had decided to move overseas, not them. I had decided for our family to become missionaries, not them. They were just babies and never had a say in where we'd be raising them. I did. I cried uncontrollably as I thought, *God, I'm ruining my kids.*

I am telling this story to say that my kids never got to choose their lives. And when we look at pictures of our life, they might bring up all kinds of feelings and memories—some good, some bad. Perhaps some feelings create personal anger toward God. *God, why did you give me this life? I never asked to be poor! I never asked my dad to abandon my siblings and me so he could kill himself working eighty hours a week—all for us to live in a big house!* And these are all things we don't get to choose when we come into this world. However, we do get to decide how we'll respond to these life events. Charles Swindoll once said, "Life is ten percent what happens to me and ninety percent how I react to it."

I can attest that God knows best what we need, even when it comes to our family. Today, at forty-three years old, I can look back and see why God chose me for my family. Or should I say, why He chose my family for me—specifically, the reason why He gave me my mom and dad.

Let me start at the beginning, at least, the beginning that I now know. My grandparents on my dad's side and great-grandparents on my mom's side came to this country as immigrants. I know very little of how my mom's side of the family transitioned into the United States. However, I know about my dad's parents and their transition, mostly because of my inquisitive nature and experiences as a kid.

My maternal grandparents would take my sister and me on day trips in the car. We loved to visit their house, and we spent a lot of time together. Grandpop Joe was once an entrepreneur VW body shop owner. After many years of the daily grind, he sold his business and took over as the caretaker of a non-profit park, Soupy Island, that provided summer fun to inner-city, underprivileged kids. My grandparents provided soup donated by Campbells, milk and crackers, and days of fun in the sun with pools, slides, swings, and one of the oldest carousels in America. My maternal grandparents were very active in church, and my grandpop always served in leadership-type roles. He was a follower of Jesus Christ with a firm belief in the Pentecostal experience. My grandpop spent time with the Lord every morning around 5 AM, whether he was walking the park or confined to the house because of rain. I realized my grandpop knew Jesus!

Grandpop Joe knew his Bible, and he devoured it daily. He knew how to pray, and if you spoke with people who knew him, they'd say he knew how to hear from God. He carried a Gideon Bible in his shirt pocket at all times. This very evening as we sat at the dinner table, my daughter shared how he always said, "I have a word for you from God," while taking that little Bible out of his shirt pocket. He loved to say, "Aaaaamen." You couldn't have a conversation without hearing it at least once.

Now yes, you're right; words and beliefs don't make us followers of Christ. What makes us Christ-followers is the daily decision to become more and more like Jesus. If we went through my grandpop's life with a fine-toothed comb, I'm sure we'd find faults. We'd find he made mistakes with his children, in living his life, and even raising his family. As grandchildren, we don't often see those faults, but they were there. Each of his kids knew of things, both right and wrong. They are the ones who have their subjective experience of growing up with him. At the same time, they will have to evaluate those experiences and choose whether they too will follow in his footsteps in navigating life while following Jesus.

Interestingly, everyone knew that my grandpop Joe had an intimate relationship with Jesus, but I never recalled a conversation about how he heard from Jesus. He never explained how to hear from God—he just did, and you knew that there was something special between him and Jesus. So how did he attempt to get Jesus into us as grandkids? I can still remember when my cousins and I were dragged around weekend after weekend to sing in nursing homes. Grandpop Joe bought cassette tapes, and we had to memorize song after song about themes such as "I am a Promise." The lyrics molded me without realizing it with words such as, "I can go anywhere that He (God) wants me to go, I can be anything that He (God) wants me to be."[3] And then there was "Beloved, let us love one another."[4] The lyrics engraved 1 John 4:7-8 into my spirit. But not just me, also into each of my cousins.

I am the only one in my family who made a conscious decision to follow Jesus into ministry. Could it be that God spoke to my grandpop and said, "Joe, one day Bobby will serve Me as a public communicator of the gospel, and you need to prepare him. Make him comfortable singing or speaking in front of people because he'll be going to the nations, and I need him comfortable as a public speaker." I never had that conversation with my grandpop. Perhaps I'm inventing something that never happened, but I know God was preparing me for missions. He was preparing me to hear His voice.

Maybe, just maybe, my grandpop thought he didn't need to teach his grandkids a programmatic way of hearing God but realized that if he could get God's word into them, God would find a way to speak. I have no idea if that was his thinking; however, this story illustrates my first understanding of how to hear God: get God's word inside you, and He will find a way to use it to speak to you.

Friends, when God's Word is in you, it will speak in its time —the proper time—of God's message to you. When I have heard from God, I can tell you that it often happened through a verse that seemed to somehow magically taken on life inside of me. I may have pondered a verse a thousand times, but when God says it's time, the verse comes alive, and I understand something that I never did before. In theological circles, we call this experience the Rhema or Logos Word of God.

> ...a Rhema is a specific word from the Lord for individual Christians. This word releases faith to take action. Often, the Holy Spirit will speak to Christians of the Living Word (logos) through the written word (graphe) which will provide a revealed word (rhema) to give guidance or release power. All three of the different manifestations of the Word are necessary and available for the believing Christian.[5]

Maybe Grandpop Joe never overtly taught me how to hear

God; maybe he did. I witnessed him read God's Word on many occasions, but beyond reading, he quoted the Scriptures repeatedly. He repeated them to me often in casual conversations. And you know what he taught me without teaching me? Read God's Word, get it inside of you, engrave it in you, and when God is ready, in His time, he will release the power of the Word.

Maybe God gave you godly examples to follow. Awesome! There's a high likelihood that you may connect with God. Or perhaps your family is far from Christianity. With no examples for us to imitate, understanding what it means to follow Jesus may seem a total impossibility.

That would be a statement my dad could give you. He and my mom grew up on opposite sides of the railroad line. Mom grew up in Palmyra, New Jersey, while dad grew up in the slum projects of Philadelphia. She was from the suburbs, whereas Dad grew up in a neighborhood where it was a case of either learn how to fight or spend your days getting bullied and beaten. What led to my dad's home situation and dangerous childhood can be traced back to his father's transition into United States life.

My paternal grandparents were immigrants. Grandpop Dezi was the first of his siblings to leave Cuba as the revolution began to overtake the country. He grew up in a family of dentists, and money was never an issue. He was the youngest of the family and spoiled in many ways by his parents. By the time the revolution hit in 1959, the government had taken control of everything—properties, bank accounts; everything had become the government property. It was soon decided that my grandpop would be sent to the United States, along with his family's maid. Even though he traveled with their maid, he had no money because of the revolution. No one was allowed to leave Cuba legally unless his or her belongings remained in Cuba as property of the State. The Cuban government restricted travel to the clothes you were wearing. So many families were divided during this era. Those who left Cuba were seen as *gusanos* (worms or traitors). The stigma surrounding leaving Cuba not only affected the individuals leaving the island but also their families. Those who remained in Cuba were bullied because their family members decided to leave the country. I don't know what life was like for my aunts and uncles when my grandpop left, but if history teaches us anything, it leads me to believe that he made their lives much harder.

Grandpop Dezi arrived in the United States as a young, poor Cuban who couldn't speak or understand English. He met my grandmom at immigration while they were learning to speak English. They fell in love, married eventually, and became parents to five kids. The poverty situation of the family overwhelmed my grandpop, driving him to become a severe alcoholic for many years. His situation soon led to him finding subpar work at a bubble gum factory.

Think about it. You grow up in the lap of luxury only to find yourself poor, young, and in a foreign country one day. It must have been a rude awakening. While I never experienced this side of my grandpop, people say he was beyond abusive with all his kids. His children were abused and beaten with extension cords or belts. There was much external evidence of what happened at home, but they lived in extreme poverty in a neighborhood where schools played no active role in protecting their pupils.

Thankfully, Grandpop Dezi eventually found his way to sobriety. I still vividly remember visiting him in the nursing home. We talked about him meeting Jesus. I then prayed with him, believing that he was coherent enough to pray the prayer of salvation. While I am thankful for that day, it could not change the years of abuse my dad experienced at the hands of his father. Fortunately, I never had to live through what my dad experienced. Still, his story would play a crucial role in my development as a child, teenager, and adult. My dad's story, while very different from mine, would become intertwined with mine.

Racism was heated during those years in Philadelphia. Dad's family was the only white family living in all-black projects. With the races widely divided and increasing racial violence, life was brutal, much like what we witness across our country today. Many of us may never understand how racism affects people on an individual basis. Although we don't understand, it doesn't mean it doesn't happen.

Grandpop Dezi and Grandmom Erna were limited in speaking English, yet they tried to raise their kids as Americans because they understood the reality of racism. They didn't live out their native-born culture and only spoke English at home. To this day, I'm the only grandchild who is bilingual. Immigrants usually bring their cultural customs with them, but that didn't happen in my family's case. Everyone abandoned their cultural norms and adopted Unites States cultural practices.

My Grandmom Erna had a religious upbringing, a characteristic that she tried to keep alive despite the many challenges at home. At times, Grandpop Dezi would steal money from her to buy liquor and then beat his kids while blaming the theft on them. At one point, Child Services had to intervene. Still, my grandmom did what she could to protect her kids. She attended various churches in Philadelphia. Of that time, Dad remarked, "Come rain or shine, Mom had all five kids on the trolley to make their way to church every Sunday."

Life didn't treat my father well. God allowed him to go through some painful situations beyond his control. Suffering abuse at the hand of family members and escaping from State care caused him to want only to leave home. I'm not sure I could trust God the way he eventually did, knowing that God saw and still permitted the things he went through. But Dad found himself in church, a place so different from anything he experienced at home. He eventually found a Palmyra girl from the other side of the bridge, a world away from his reality. He fell in love with her and became part of a new family. After he and Mom were married, he made sure they lived on the Jersey side of the Philadelphia bridge, as far away from the projects as possible. Both Mom and Dad had to learn how to evolve as parents and learn what it meant for them to follow Jesus.

More amazing is that Dad, with only a limited formal education, became one of the top Volvo mechanics on the East coast. Growing up, he became competent at fixing just about everything, a Cuban trait he somehow inherited. He fixed houses, cars, appliances, and never paid anyone to do work for him. He managed to do all of this at a time without YouTube or Google. Amazing. One time while learning to plumb, he dug a three-foot trench around the entire side of our house only to discover that Mom clogged our sewage line right by the street. I was probably more of a nuisance than anything, but I followed him around porting tools, thinking that I, too, could help fix everything. The truth is, all I did was create more work for him.

I don't believe it was by accident that my dad became one of the best Volvo mechanics on the East coast. He inherited a Cuban trait that permeated his life more than even he understood. Cubans are extraordinary at creating something out of nothing. For decades, they have made futures with limited resources out of necessity. There was just something in Dad that gave him the ability to succeed even though everything around him said, "You're never going to succeed! You have nothing; you're nothing. You've lived in poverty all your life; you only have a limited Philadelphia school education, and your family is not so much the picture of perfection. Bob, give up already." There was always a voice in my dad that let him know that he didn't have to get beaten up because he was the minority in his neighborhood. A voice somehow pushed him to believe he could make it, a voice that said his kids would live different lives. And you know what, we did!

My sister and I grew up as suburban kids, visiting my grandparents only on weekends. We played soccer, attended good schools, and engaged in many extracurricular activities because of my parents' sacrifices. We had all of the opportunities my parents never had. Why? Because they believed! They believed it was possible because of a voice that never spoke audibly but internally— even if they never heard it.

What do I mean? Whereas my maternal grandpop Joe lived out the importance of getting God's word inside of you and allowing it to speak, my dad, Bob, taught me indirectly that God puts natural inclinations in every one of us. These natural inclinations give important clues to God's design for where we should pursue our involvement in His kingdom. We may not always get it right, but part of following God is listening very intently to those natural inclinations.

Natural Inclinations

In 2015, a couple of missionaries came to Costa Rica to work with me. The couple came from Texas. Their ministry experience was limited, but I felt a genuine connection with the husband as we sat down for lunch one day. I asked how they could help in ministry, and we talked for hours. He told me a story that day of a guy with little to no ministry experience but with a talent for construction, a characteristic that I desperately needed because of my many projects. I soon invited them to work with us in Costa Rica. I intentionally decided to move them out of their comfort zones so they could experience many other facets of ministry. I wanted them to discover in that process where their natural inclinations would make them feel most effective.

I've learned God's voice expresses itself in our natural inclinations for ministry. Often, our ideal place for serving God in ministry is closely connected to our natural inclinations. For example, this Texan man found he felt most at home when he was engaged with construction. God can speak without ever having to use words! We just have to be sensitive enough to listen. My job was to help position this man in a way that would allow him to connect with God's voice. I did that by helping him explore ministry regarding the things he liked and disliked.

We can miss God's voice if we push an agenda or if we don't reflect on God's role in our lives. We must stop to consider our activities and how God might be speaking through them.

The concept of natural inclinations doesn't mean I'm advocating an ideology of liberalism—the idea that we can do whatever we want as long as it feels good. The God-given natural inclinations that line up with your God-given call will always be in sync with God's Word. As Martin Luther succinctly said, "The Bible...supplies the true and sound doctrine." Luther believed that Scripture interprets Scripture. For those natural inclinations to be number one, from God, they can't go against Scripture. Furthermore, 2 Timothy 3:16 plainly states, "All Scripture is God-breathed and is useful for teaching, rebuking, correcting and training in righteousness." Whenever He speaks, no matter the method, God ensures that His words always align with biblical precedence.

God has given each of us a story. Maybe we've decided to follow Jesus or maybe not, but it doesn't change the fact that we all have a story, and God desires to be a part of that story. There will be inconceivable stories in some people's lives, and there may also be stories of pure bliss in other people's lives. We don't get to choose these stories the same way we don't choose our family. That's why it's so important, regardless of where we find ourselves within our narratives, to allow God to write through our story. We must be careful to look for pieces of Him in us. If you'll pay attention closely, you'll notice that there are desires that God Himself put in you.

As a boy, I visited my paternal grandparents on weekends. As my parents sought to discover my natural inclinations in life, they found I had a talent for art. I loved to draw. On my bedroom wall was a life-sized, hand-painted bull representing the Chicago Bulls I had painted. An art table sat in the corner of my room, with paper and drawing supplies. I spent hours at that table. To encourage that gift, my parents enrolled me at the Moore College of Art on the weekends. My grandpop and I took the 'El train' into downtown Philadelphia every weekend so I could attend art classes. Some classmates were destined to be professional. During these trips, I grew closer to my grandpop, and somewhere along the way, I also developed a passion for understanding his life growing up in Cuba.

Believe it or not, as a little boy, God put two very real desires in my heart. The first was that I wanted to learn to speak Spanish at all costs. As a kid, I got my hands on Spanish books and taught myself. I badgered my grandpop to try to get him to teach me. I wasn't successful at getting Grandpop to help, but I was very successful with the books I read. I learned a lot, and even though my Spanish was very bad, by the time I was eighteen, I could hold a conversation by speaking very broken Spanish.

The second desire was that I wanted to marry a Puerto Rican girl. I really don't know why; I only knew there was something inside of me with a strong desire to marry a Puerto Rican. Not Colombian, Cuban, Costa Rican, or anything else, but a Puerto Rican woman. And so, this keen interest developed in my spirit toward Cuba and Puerto Rico. These innate desires weren't something I conjured up; they were simply there for as long as I could remember.

Not all innate desires or cravings are from God. If we're going to attribute anything as being from God, it must first be established with Scripture! We can't ignore this invaluable point. We were all born in a natural state separated from God. In addition, we all live in a broken world. These two truths are the primary reasons everyone will struggle with desires that were never born out of God's design. This is exactly why 1 John 2:15-17 (NLT) admonishes us with the following advice:

> Do not love this world nor the things it offers you, for when you love the world, you do not have the love of the Father in you. For the world offers only a craving for physical pleasure, a craving for everything we see, and pride in our achievements and possessions. These are not from the Father but are from this world. And this world is fading away, along with everything that people crave. But anyone who does what pleases God will live forever.

The apostle John would have us understand that belonging to the world leads to cravings that are altogether alien to the personality of Christ. Everyone falls into this category. Unless we've decided to follow Jesus, we will, from birth, struggle with cravings that further separate us from God. On the other hand, while deciding to follow Jesus doesn't make us immune to these cravings, it does open the door for God to deposit new desires within us.

Regardless of who you are, you'll never be immune to the pull of earthly cravings! Some might say, "Well then, what is the point of committing ourselves to Christ if He will not eliminate those human, fleshly, earthly desires and cravings?" The point is that He wants us to want Him. He wants us to depend on His daily bread or daily sustenance. Christianity without recognition for the need of God makes us dependent on ourselves. Jesus made it clear, "Here on earth you will have many trials and sorrows. But take heart, because I have overcome the world" (John 16:33 NLT). Jesus has overcome, and He will help us to overcome. This must be a daily overcoming as an ongoing decision to try once again to rely on Jesus. When that becomes our habit, we create opportunities for God to create cravings that will bring us closer and closer to becoming like Jesus and fulfilling His will.

Whoever has ears, let them hear (Matt. 11:15 NLT)

MY HOLY SPIRIT MOMENT

Without the Spirit of God, we can do nothing. We are as ships without wind. We are useless. – Charles Spurgeon

By the time I moved into adolescence, I didn't recognize God as being intricately involved in writing my story. Like so many other teenagers, I had to go through a discovery phase that lasted for far too many years. It wasn't until I grew up, had kids, and struggled with being a parent that I finally realized the heartache I caused my parents when I was just a dumb kid.

I was about 38-years-old when I called my mom from Costa Rica and said, "Mom, I just want to say sorry. I caused you and Daddy a lot of heartache when I was a teenager, and I'm sorry. I'm sorry I was so rebellious."

Naturally, my mom said, "You don't need to apologize. You were fine; you weren't that bad."

That's what we do as parents. We love beyond the pain, the fights, the arguments. I'd argue that it's no different with God. As Romans 3:23 says, "For everyone has sinned; we all fall short of God's glorious standard." Yet, God already knows the magnitude of each of our sins and is determined to create a way for forgiveness. God made a path to Him that couldn't be earned, bought, nor negotiated. This path would be available to all; that way was through Jesus and Him alone.

If we're honest, it's not always the easiest thing to submit fully to Jesus. Whether we're teenagers, young adults, or even seasoned life-long Christians, we'll all eventually run into circumstances where we'll grapple with that decision on a personal level.

My teenage years were full of many of those decisions. Unfortunately, I didn't always get it right, but that's what I genuinely love about the Bible. God never chose to hide the human struggle. So many times, we hear people question the veracity of the Bible. If God were worried about getting people on board with the Bible, He would have hidden the failures of which we read. Think of how tempting it would have been for God, or even the biblical authors for that matter, to gloss over the fact that within our Savior's lineage was recorded evidence of a harlot. Ray Pritchard says, "This genealogy is in the Bible to let us know that he had a background a lot like yours and mine. He called himself 'the friend of sinners,' and he said he didn't come to call the righteous, but sinners to repentance."[6] We find references to problems with anger (Moses), infidelity (David), and conflict (Paul and Barnabas), to name a few. The Bible is a story of real life. It's a story that connects with our human nature while at the same time demonstrates the need for a Savior who was "tempted in every way, just as we are—yet he didn't sin" (Hebrews 4:15).

During my younger years, our family attended various churches. Two churches that stand out in my memory are the Church of God in Gloucester City and the Assembly of God church in Blackwood, New Jersey. During those years, I attended a Baptist school. I couldn't stand that school. Yes, I admit it. It was actually my fault because I was constantly talking. I was often in trouble, in detention, or in the principal's office. While I had some good friends, it didn't change the fact that the school experience was not very enjoyable. My sister ended up staying and graduating from there, but I managed to convince my parents to take me out and enroll me in the local public school. Interestingly enough, I hated the public school even more. Isn't it funny how sometimes the things we fight for end up being the things we hate? Life so often happens like that.

But here's what happened. Before leaving the Baptist school, I experienced what Pentecostals refer to as baptism in the Holy Spirit. That moment is something I vividly remember. At the time, I was attending the Assembly of God church. The church held special revival services in those days that very few of today's young people will ever experience. The church intentionally sought to create an environment for people to encounter the Holy Spirit intimately. These included tarrying moments at the altar.

The Holy Spirit was Someone I had openly heard about but never personally experienced. I knew my Grandpop Joe was one of those Holy Spirit experiencing people. He had his prayer times in the early morning and often prayed in a strange language known as tongues. He believed the words of 1 Corinthians 4:18, where Paul said he was a proud tongues speaker. This experience was foreign to me.

That would change. Why? Because God wanted me to understand that this experience wasn't for a select few. He wanted me to experience this language known as tongues. He wanted me to experience Him. My future decision to enter missions would be intricately connected to my own Holy Spirit moment.

Paul wrote letters to the early church emphasizing the importance of "spiritual gifts" (1 Corinthians 12). He didn't want the Corinthian church to be uninformed regarding these gifts (1 Corinthians 12:1) because there's something special about God's power. God desires for us to experience this power as followers of Christ. Think about what Acts 1:8 meant to the early church as it started to grow. Jesus was just as clear as Paul when He said His people were going to spread His message (Matthew 28:16-20). However, He wanted them to wait until they were endued with a divine power that would come from God in the person of the Holy Spirit.

The gifts of the Holy Spirit that we read about in 1 Corinthians were manifesting themselves in my church, and I was intrigued. I was just a kid, but I was intrigued.

We had a youth group of 30 to 50 kids. We were a tight-knit

community of students. Some students were really searching to understand whether God was for them, while others actively pursued what it would look like to know God. We went to those Holy Spirit church services. I saw and even heard some things that shocked me. People sang, laughed, sometimes fell down; the experiences varied. Still, it didn't take a rocket scientist to know that something was there—something that was possibly divine. At this stage, I began to ask God, "Can I also speak in tongues like these church people?" Service after service, I closed my eyes, talked to God, and tried to believe that He would touch me the way He touched other people, but it didn't happen. I became discouraged. It was probably a good thing that I was born a stubborn kid. It took a lot for me to accept failure. If you were to ask my wife, she'd tell you that not much has changed.

One weekend in particular really challenged me personally. A traveling evangelist who preached in different churches came to our area. His wife was dying of cancer, and she somehow came to live with my family during her cancer journey. Because of this situation, he spoke more than usual at my home church. It seemed like a divine, holy move of God whenever this man shared at my church. It led to me getting serious with God in a real way, serious enough to ask Him to allow me to experience this baptism in the Holy Spirit and speak in other tongues. Sadly though, it seemed like my search to experience the Pentecostal experience was never going to result in anything substantive.

Now, remember, I attended a faith-based school. That meant that we were required to participate in Bible class. And that's where my church and school worlds collided. Some areas of the church world think that the experiences witnessed by those in the primitive church ceased to exist a long time ago. Some believe that these Holy Spirit experiences were essential to the establishment of the early church, but they have since ceased to function since the completion of the Bible.[7] Now some people who believe this "cessationist-based" theory are great God-fearing Christ-followers. I have the utmost respect for them. Furthermore, they have a great understanding of the

Bible. However, when it came to the gifts of the Spirit found in 1 Corinthians 12, for some reason, I wasn't satisfied with what I was being taught in school. Something inside of me drove me to want more, to believe that I, too, could experience this intimate relationship with the Holy Spirit as evidenced by speaking in other tongues.

So what should a twelve-year-old boy do who is told one thing but seems to feel the inner conviction of another? Even though I didn't understand it, I challenged the system. I questioned my teachers. I couldn't simply conform. And this is the human experience. Or maybe I should say the teenage experience! For just a moment, think about what Lindsay Hawkes (Focus on the Family Contributor) says:

> As a parent, you've invested your life in your child. You brought them to church, taught them everything you know about the Bible, and prayed with them at night. You wanted nothing but God's absolute best for their life. Then, almost before you knew it, your son or daughter morphed into a teenager and dropped a startling confession on you: I'm not interested in going to church and I'm not sure if I believe that the Bible is true. I don't know if God is real, or why I should believe in Him. Every situation is unique, but the gist of the scenario is the same: your child is wrestling with their faith. [8]

All teenagers wrestle with rebelliousness to some degree. We must wrestle with our faith as we mature into adulthood. We'll struggle multiple times with our faith in following God or maturing into Christ-followers. Do I believe? Do I not believe? Will I follow? Will I pay the price needed to follow Jesus? These are all great questions, and they must be dealt with if we're going to follow Jesus long-term.

Perhaps you have never been allowed to question your faith, your belief in the God of the Bible. Maybe you have even felt guilty about doubting, and the list here could go on and on. This struggling with our faith is so biblical. The struggle in following God's call on our life is biblical. Even Jesus struggled. As Jesus prepared to go to the cross where He was to die a horrendous death, He said to God, "Father, if you are willing, please take this cup of suffering away from me. Yet I want your will to be done, not mine" (Luke 22:42). He wasn't afraid to express His profound anguish, pain, and fear of what lay ahead.

People have taught us to fear expressing our biggest faith hang-ups. They have taught us to hide them, maybe even to lie to ourselves about them because they have failed to look at the whole context of the Bible. By teaching words, verses, chapters, and even books out of their original biblical context, people have instilled beliefs in us that are not right. Moses stuttered, and he made sure God knew he thought himself incapable; Gideon asked for sign after sign because he struggled to believe. Peter fought an incredible internal battle that would play out before the world on the pages of the Bible as he too denied his Savior! So, I challenge you to find a place of solitude, sit with God, and allow yourself to feel, guilt free, whatever causes you to struggle in your faith. And then share it with God. Trust me; He will not get mad, upset, or angry with you.

There were moments in my life when I pushed against formal religion. I can remember putting my parents through some dreadful struggles because I, too, had to figure out who God was. Somehow, I emerged on the other side of my struggles, believing God's truth. Maybe it's just me, but I just have never been able to believe because someone simply told me something. The Bible encourages us to engage in the kind of thinking that causes us to study the Scriptures to show ourselves approved (2 Timothy 2:15). I remember thinking, specifically about this whole baptism in the Spirit, that God didn't want to give it to me! I remember thinking, *I'm not worthy*. But I still couldn't accept my Bible teacher pushing a "cessation" theology without me questioning the validity of that teaching because of what I witnessed at my church.

I don't believe in ascribing to beliefs based on subjective-experiential moments without a biblical supporting foundation. We do this way too often, and we must make sure we're grounded in the Scriptures above all. One day in Bible class, we spoke about the topic of the Holy Spirit. During the class, the dialogue revolved around understanding the meaning of Scriptures and their current-day relevancy. I, for one, didn't speak in other tongues, although I was still fervently seeking that experience. My best friend and classmate, Lenny Santiago, was a Pentecostal believer. He was a practicing Christ-follower who had experienced speaking in other tongues. Naturally, he influenced me and my thinking. So, when he went to town defending his faith experience, I tried to support Lenny and add some additional perspectives to the conversation. Well, I failed! I failed miserably, and my teacher obviously defended his own stance. When school ended that day, I got into the car and cried internally all the way home. I felt as though God had abandoned me. I was defending something I hadn't experienced, and I came away looking foolish.

Just when you thought that was the end of the story, God did something unique. I went into my room, closed the door, knelt by the side of my bed, and began to cry out loud. "God," I asked, "Am I not worthy? Why won't you baptize me in the Holy Spirit? I even defended it in class, having never experienced it myself. Why?" Amid my tears, my complaining, and even my questioning of the Holy Spirit's existence, God did something supernatural. I opened my mouth to speak again, probably to make another complaint, when words suddenly came out of my mouth that I had never heard before. There was no special God cloud, no visible manifestation of God, but all of a sudden, I began to speak in what Pentecostal people call "other tongues" – the baptism in the Holy Spirit. I was so scared, I stopped speaking. Then I thought, *Maybe if I go outside and open my mouth, it will continue to flow.* That's what I did. I went out back, still in shock. When I opened my mouth to begin to speak again, this language of God started to roll off my tongue.

Why did God wait so long? Or better yet, what would have happened in my life-long journey of following Jesus had the circumstances been different? I don't have the answer, but I know that faith in Jesus Christ is not blind faith. Christianity is not—nor will ever be—blind faith. The Bible is full of stories that will challenge our faith and our commitment to follow Jesus. Those stories help to develop a faith within us that's rooted in experience. The writer of Hebrews (11:1) challenged us to have a faith that sees beyond what can be seen, but he never intended for us to have "blind" faith. He intended that our faith would rest upon a God who has proven himself over and over throughout the pages of history.

MY YEARS AS A YOUTH

...there is spiritual courage—the willingness to ask the deep questions about God, existence, meaning, death, and life after death. Many people spend their entire lives avoiding these questions, putting them off until some later date "when I have more time" or "when I'm old and closer to death." But all of life is preparation for death. We have been given this life so that we may prepare ourselves for the life to come.[9]

Fast forward a few years, and you'll begin to see how God had been preparing me internally in terms of my family, circumstances, and natural inclinations. He began to orchestrate my life in a way that would allow me to experience Him, His provisions, and His plan for my life in an incredible, unthinkable way.

My youth, just like anyone else's, was full of both good and bad experiences. For a few years, I even chose to step away from my faith. You go to high school and experience the influences, and tribes start emerging between the students. You really have to work hard to figure out who you are, and sometimes the process isn't pretty. I'm fortunate that I never became a slave to the vices that destroy so many teens. I can't explain why God chose to deal with me as He did, but there was something about teenage Bob that would never allow him to get away with anything without getting caught. I was caught every time I tried to break the law or engage in an illicit activity.

Working Out My Faith

I could fill the next few pages with numerous stories of my

attempted rebellion. My mom and dad could probably entertain you with story after story of how their son tried to be prodigal with little success. They'd tell you about Chopper (another story for another time), how I was beaten up, or how I snuck out with music playing in my room, only for Dad to catch me on his way home from work. You'll learn how God set up an encounter with a girl from Camden who truly changed my life. And if my mom told you the story, she'd tell you I was on a three-month parent-mandated house arrest when that set-up encounter happened. She'd even tell you how she hung up the phone on the girl God was planning on using to correct my path.

But here's the moral of the story: I had to work out my faith! I had to figure out whether I wanted to follow Jesus personally or spend a lifetime running in rebellion. My faith is an ongoing process. Honestly, I can't say that I've ever fully worked it out. Still, there have been significant moments in my life when God divinely intervened to position me to receive from Him, even without my understanding. It has been said, "Experience is not the best teacher; evaluated experience is." We may not see, sense, or hear God in the moment, but when we look back at our lives and evaluate our experiences, we begin to see and recognize God. I believe He intentionally works in the background while we're going through everyday life moments. That way, we'll consciously take time to reflect, meditate, understand, and then choose to see Him or ourselves as the designer of our life story. The following point is important: God is a jealous God. Just read the Old Testament, and you'll see that God was jealous for His people. He wanted to be seen and recognized by His people.

As I sit here and intentionally reflect, you know what I see? I see a God who was interested. He had no reason to be. What's more, there was never a guarantee that I'd believe God was positioning me to receive friends into my life who would spur me on in my eventual pursuit of God. For some of you, your family or kids may never make an ALTO (stop) and choose to recognize God, but that will never, ever stop His interest in you or them.

For example, remember how God put a desire in me to marry

a Puerto Rican girl? Well, it was that desire and that girl who would connect me with those friends and with God.

Let me explain. My church participated in monthly youth rallies, which involved many church youth groups getting together. Those events had two purposes. The first was to create a community of the youth of South Jersey, and the second was to create an environment where young people could seek God. I'd be lying if I said I always wanted to attend those youth events. There were times I didn't want to go, but at the end of the day, I always went for two reasons.

First, my dad made me go to church whenever we had youth activities or events. My dad grew up a tough cookie. Little Bobby didn't have that same tough childhood experience. I was afraid of my dad because I knew he could beat me in a fight. Second, there were always girls! What young person wouldn't take advantage of such an opportunity?

After one of these youth events, everyone went to the Cherry Hill Skating Rink. We packed out that place. There were teenagers from all walks of life, both inner city and suburbs. Some skated, while others did nothing more than watch people skate. I wasn't the best skater, although I could defend myself fairly decently on a pair of skates. My buddies and I went out on the skating floor trying to show off by skating forward, backward, or whatever else we could do to draw attention. There were lots of girls there, and we tried hard to impress them.

Out of nowhere, to my surprise, a youth pastor approached me, trying to get my attention. I pulled over to the side, and to my amazement, he asked, "You see that girl over there? She likes you." That was it; that was all he said, at least from what I remember. Then he just walked away. I thought to myself, *How odd*. Then I thought, *Jackpot!* That girl's youth group was the loudest and most outspoken group. They were the most inner-city group, but when I saw the girl the youth pastor told me about, I realized she was one of the most beautiful girls there. And she was Puerto Rican.

Little did I know that God was designing my destiny in a

skating rink at a church event my dad forced me to attend. Thanks, Dad! Naturally, I approached her, but I did it in a very suave way. That night I was dressed to impress, or so I thought. I had a yellow-and-orange striped shirt with hot yellow pants and purple Patrick Ewing shoes. It looked like someone put batteries in my clothes. Thank God, I've matured in my style since I was a fifteen-year-old.

I walked over to this fourteen-year-old girl, but rather than being formal and saying, "Hi, how are you?" I blurted out, "So, I hear you like me." That's no way to start a conversation with a girl, but she was not phased. I don't remember what she said, but I know she made a face, responded in a like manner, and gave me a smart retort. When I finally did ask her name, I tried to impress her by saying her last name, Mercado, but in a way (like rolling the "r") that would let her know I was a Spanish fan. We talked for a little while until I finally dropped the question, "Can I get your number?" Her response was, "I don't have a phone." *Who doesn't have a phone?* I thought. We were just kids; it wasn't like I could drive over to her house. Still, I kept pushing to call her until she finally said, "Well, there's a payphone in front of my house at the corner. I can call you from there." Again, jackpot. So I gave her some money to call me.

But the problem was, she never called me. I don't think my Spanish technique worked. What's more, not only did I find out that her friends made fun of me on the way back home that night, but they were cracking jokes about my name and me being Caucasian. They told this girl that I was a white guy from the suburbs, and there was no way she should even consider giving me the time of day.

All the cards were stacked against me. It was a zero-sum game; at least that's how I could have let the story play out. God used my youthful naivete, the innocence of my youth, to His advantage. That girl decided not to call me because she let her friends talk her out of following her heart (or so I like to think). She lived in the inner city of Camden; I was from the suburbs. Her family had no car and no phone, so a relationship wasn't going to work.

The only reason she went to church was because of an elderly gentleman named Brother Leonard. Every Wednesday and Sunday, he'd faithfully get to church early and drive the streets of Camden to pick up anyone who needed a ride. Thanks, Brother Leonard! My only thought was, *You better believe I'm going to be at the next youth event.* She wasn't getting rid of me that easily.

However, that next church event was never necessary. I convinced my mom to take me shopping for clothes at a place called Forman Mills. We didn't usually shop there. The clothes were knock-offs, not the best quality, but they were in my style. In Mom's motherly way, she was willing to indulge me and take me shopping there. As I browsed the aisles, that girl's brother spotted me and told his sister, "That corny white guy is here."

Again, we were face-to-face, and I never gave one thought that she might not like me. There's almost a beauty in youth naivete. When we haven't fully experienced life yet, we're more often open to new experiences. We're more open to taking risks because we haven't learned yet of the pitfalls that befall us because of our decisions. And believe it or not, it worked. By the end of the conversation, she invited me to go with her youth group to Six Flags Great Adventure Park. There was still the phone issue, but she promised to call me, and she did.

God orchestrates events even when we're oblivious to His working. I had no idea back then who this girl was going to be in my life. Who would have thought that God could set me up to meet a girl at a clothes outlet when I was just a teenager? That encounter only happened because God deposited certain natural inclinations in me as a young boy. Because of God, by the time I was a teenager, He was already making a way for me to meet this one-of-a-kind Puerto Rican girl from the inner city of Camden. I didn't recognize it as God's plan back then, but I sure do now. That girl was Michele Mercado, now Pérez, my high school sweetheart, and my one and only wife.

She told me from the very beginning, "I can't date you if you're not a Christian." That was a pretty bold move on her part. Maybe she was trying to get rid of me, I don't know, but she marked the "cancha" (field) plainly and clearly. If you're a teenager and a beautiful girl likes you and makes a bold statement like that, you get saved, baptized, and become a Christ-follower all in sixty seconds. But seriously, I was infatuated with this girl. I was going to do whatever it took to be with her. Although we were kids, God was working with us in ways that are sometimes beyond our comprehension. Our relationship blossomed, and somehow, the church was always at the center of everything we did. I asked my mom if I could attend a youth group with Michele at her church in Pennsauken. So, after agreeing, Mom drove me to Michele's house every Wednesday so I could get on the inner-city church bus. Not only did I get to be with Michele, but God set me on a path that would allow me to experience Him and His call in a spectacular way.

A gradual rekindling of the Holy Spirit started to occur within me. I felt as though God always remembered me! Recalling the Old Testament narrative, I realized that's essentially God's modus operandi. Regardless of where we find ourselves in relation to God, He always remembers us. Israel repeatedly walked away from God, yet the Scriptures show us how God continually sought to restore that relationship. Jesus stepped out of heaven onto earth as a perfect, sinless lamb in the greatest demonstration of care to repair that relationship. Scriptures tell of the fantastic indwelling of the Holy Spirit that will take place if we respond to His sacrifice for us and follow in the footsteps of Jesus Christ. The Father sends His Holy Spirit to advocate, teach, give peace, empower, and so much more (John 14:25-27; Acts 1:8).

Little did I know that I was about to embark on a journey of seeking and experiencing God. I didn't simply want to know about Him; instead, I wanted to experience Him in all His fullness. Just think of Moses's continual experience as the Israelites marched through the wilderness. He stepped into a tent, and God always showed up. The people knew God was there because of the cloud that covered the tent. Led by a fire at night and a cloud by day, Israel was hydrated by a rock and fed by a supernatural food called manna. At one point, Moses found himself on the side of a mountain, shielded from seeing God's face, but wholly surrounded by God's goodness (Exodus 33:21-23).

Oh, how I long for moments like these—moments when my faith is invigorated by a biblical understanding that leads to a beautiful, unforgettable, experiential understanding. Many may have individual, distinct experiences with God, and those moments will almost undoubtedly leave an impressionable mark upon their lives. We can choose to forget those moments with God as the Israelites did so many times. However, we can also choose to allow these life-changing moments to gradually build upon one another, taking us to higher heights with Him in life, in prayer, and in our walk with God.

This is precisely what was happening with me. God was shaping my life in particular ways, and these marks were beginning to build upon one another. Whether I was being baptized in the Holy Spirit, meeting my high school sweetheart, connecting with a church as a part of our evolving friendship or relationship, or any of the other God-moments I experienced, God was using life to speak to me, even if I couldn't hear Him at the time.

The next hurdle in the process was for me to become very close friends with the youths who initially made fun of me when Michele and I first met at the skating rink. Three boys were about to become an integral part of my life. Two of them, Emmanuel and Edwin, were raised *hueso colorado* (indoctrinated to their core) by the Spanish Pentecostal church. They witnessed things I had never seen before in the church. Their experiences enlightened my understanding of the Holy Spirit. The third friend who would become very dear to my heart was Michele's little brother, Marco. For the next three years, these guys would become my "compadres" (best buds), and together, we'd all experience God in the most remarkable ways.

Because my friends didn't have a car, my mom came through in a big way. There was no way for them to leave the inner city to visit my house in the suburbs, but Mom made it possible for us to be friends. She transported us all over town, besides picking up and dropping Michele off at her house in the projects. I wonder, could it be that Mom sensed God doing something in our lives? Did she ever think God was using her to connect me with this church and these guys—and even participating in God's plan for my life? I don't know. But I know this: if it weren't for my parents, those relationships would have never flourished, nor would I've been led to understand the Holy Spirit the way I did.

The guys and I talked weekly about the supernatural aspects of God, watched TV evangelists together, and never expected any miracle or experience to be too big for God. They expected supernatural experiences to be present in church. They took every opportunity possible to make that plain for all to see. During that period, Benny Hinn became (a well-known TV evangelist) our hero of the faith, and we imitated him and other TV evangelists. The Pentecostal experience was starting to become something we desired with all of our hearts.

To illustrate our youthful fervor for wanting to experience God, I must share a relevant story that makes me laugh even to this day. One night when I was older and owned a car, we went to pick up a friend in Pennsauken. I was throwing pebbles at his bedroom window because it was late, and I knew he couldn't have company. His parents heard the noise of the rocks, which prompted them to call the police. Scared and panicked, I ran to the other side of the block. When police dogs met me, I dropped to the ground as fast as I could. We were taken to the station and put in a cell. We should have been concerned and cooperated; instead, the four of us started re-enacting Paul and Silas in prison. We sang to the top of our voices—only the doors weren't shaken, nor did they open. Needless to say, the police weren't happy, and neither was my mom when she picked me up.

One time, I convinced my mom to take us to Virginia to participate in a Benny Hinn crusade at the 700 Club headquarters. Before that day, I had only seen the phenomenon of people slain in the Spirit on TV or in limited church settings. I had never had that experience. To my amazement, Benny Hinn called me up to the stage that evening. When he blew in my direction, he said, "Good night." I'll never forget that moment. It was as if someone grabbed my shirt and threw me on the floor! It was unmistakable —and not one person had touched me. It was purely supernatural.

That day marked me.

We returned home to New Jersey, blown away by the move of God that took place in that arena. We heard that an evangelist was coming from New York to hold a short crusade nearby in North Camden, and we just knew we had to be there.

The church building was ragged and falling apart. It was a dilapidated home that the people had converted into a meeting place. Drugs were abundant. Crackheads, prostitutes, and every other type of needy person lived nearby. It didn't seem to be a place where you'd find God. But I did! Again, just like the Benny Hinn event, God was there. I was dumbfounded. Speechless. People worshiped the Lord that night with such enthusiasm that I'm sure the neighbors down the street heard the music. The visiting evangelist prayed for people to get healed, baptized in the Spirit, and, more importantly, saved. It seemed that people you wouldn't expect to see in church somehow found their way forward to the altar. These men and women committed their lives to Christ, but what struck me was God's presence in this unfamiliar yet exciting atmosphere. You couldn't touch it, but somehow you felt it. You knew God was there. So that night on Eighth and State Street in the inner city of Camden, I told God, "If you're genuinely real, then I want to know you. I want you to use me."

I'd love to say that God seized the opportunity and spoke to me right then and there in person. I'd love to say that the heavens opened, a voice spoke from on high, but it didn't happen that way. I often think about the call of God and how it plays out so differently in our individual lives. The writer of Matthew 4:18-19 says one of Jesus's most famous disciples, Peter, was fishing when Jesus walked by and said, "Follow me." Matthew was sitting at his tax collector kiosk when Jesus approached him and asked Matthew to follow Him (Matthew 9:9). When John the Baptist baptized Jesus (Matthew 3:16-17), we read that the Holy

Spirit descended upon Jesus in the form of a dove.

Paul, the primary writer of most of our New Testament, was a known persecutor of Christ-followers when he first encountered Jesus. Luke reveals that Paul's encounter was incredible (Acts 9). A blinding light from heaven, an audible voice heard only by Paul, and then a three-day blindness. His encounter was dramatic—life-changing. Some might say, "Off the charts!" Who wouldn't want to meet Jesus like that? However, in each case, it wasn't enough to simply hear His call. Each man, including Jesus, had to respond.

Every person's encounter is different. Some are dramatic, while others are surprisingly simplistic. There is no explanation why, but God chooses the encounter, not us. God is the one who chooses our call, not us. Furthermore, if we choose to follow in the footsteps of Jesus Christ, only we can choose our response. We can commit twenty-five, fifty, or even seventy-five percent of ourselves, but I am convinced that God asks for one hundred percent from us.

I was recently challenged in this line of thinking when Pastor Keith Conley (Harvest Assembly of God, Lakeland, Florida) said, "We've become great at doing church, but where we fail is in becoming the church." Doing church is easy. It involves church attendance, giving our finances, and going through the weekly programmed motions of what we think it means to be a Christian. But becoming the church is different. It involves change. It involves realizing God called us to be different. The early church founders were not simple church attenders; they knew they were the church and had to live accordingly!

In *Comeback Churches*, Ed Stetzer and Mike Dodson identified three characteristics often found in churches whose people are becoming the church. These "becoming the church" individuals are:

> (1) Pray-ers. Everyone can pray for the church's outreach to be effective, pray by name for those the church is trying to reach, and pray for specific outreach events.

(2) Bring-ers. Realistically, about half of the congregation will bring and include someone in a "bring a friend" day or some outreach event.

(3) Tell-ers. God has put some tell-ers in your church already, but you need your church to be made up of tell-ers.[10]

I think we all need to wrestle with this description of what it might mean to become the church. It challenges me because it encompasses the idea of responding and doing God's will regardless of how He communicates it to us.

Peter, John, Paul, and every Bible writer had an encounter with Jesus where they recognized God wanted them. How He chooses to deliver that call, whether in a specific, powerful, or simplistic way, is a God-thing. God may never verbally communicate that call, and it might be an internal natural inclination that comes to life when reading Scripture, or perhaps it occurs when speaking with a friend or hearing a song. The main thing is that it's for everyone, and we must all respond!

If you want to follow Jesus, then it must start with movement. If you spend your whole life waiting for God to give you a supernatural word or experience, you may have to wait three lifetimes. I can assure you this: God always communicates action steps. It takes time to learn to be still and listen, but there are times where we must choose movement over stagnation.

My Personal Encounter with the Holy Spirit

I had the unique experience of sensing God call me. I had hoped that when I said, "I want You to use me," it would have happened immediately. In truth, I had to wait another three months. Thankfully, when God was ready, so was I. I had been hungrily seeking God not only in public worship but also in private prayer times. My sister would whisper in the heater vents, hoping I'd think God was speaking to me. I was so naïve. In hindsight, God must have chuckled at me from His throne in heaven.

Three months later, I was in a church in Blackwood. I was on the left-hand side of the church, three pews back in the middle of a worship service. My hands lifted high when it happened. There was no explosion, no dove, no super-spectacular visual event; it was just God and me. Suddenly, it was as if God's presence enveloped me, with electricity coursing through my veins. Eyes closed and hands lifted high, I knew something was happening; something was different. It seemed as though I stood before God's presence, although I couldn't see Him.

No one around me had any idea that anything was happening. But God met me there with His presence surrounding me, and for the first time, I felt I could ask Him questions, and He would respond. I don't know how I knew I could ask God a question, and I didn't expect a verbal or audible answer, but I knew. I asked, "God, do you want me to be a missionary?" Although my eyes were still closed, it seemed as though I saw someone in the distance nodding His head in affirmation. I asked, "But where? Cuba?" (For some reason, that country burned in my heart even though I didn't know why. From childhood, I had wanted to marry a Puerto Rican and had an uncanny desire to speak Spanish. I wanted to understand more about my family's history and the country of Cuba, of which my family never spoke). Again, the head nodded yes. Then suddenly, God's presence and the electric-charged atmosphere that enveloped me vanished. I was back in church in that third pew. I was back at the Sunday morning church service that happened every week, and no one except me knew what had just happened.

Does that sound a little absurd, maybe a little ridiculous that something so out of the ordinary, so unexplainable, could be from God? Welcome to the adventure of following Jesus. Do you learn to walk on your very first step? Can you ride a bike the first time you try? So it is in following God. God is a master in providing details on a need-to-know basis.

During *The Chosen* TV series, one of the disciples asked Jesus, "How can we go to Samaria? We're Jews! Jesus, we just don't associate with Samaritans. How can we let Matthew, the tax collector, join our group? He's a Jew, yet he takes advantage of his own people and charges taxes for Rome. He's just so different!" On the show, Jesus responded, "Get used to different." Although the dialogue was added to the show for interest, I think the Jesus of the Bible would also say to us, "Get used to different."

Jesus never followed a prescribed pattern or allowed himself to be boxed in by some predetermined, prearranged method when He called people. The Jesus of the Bible might tell us as well, "Get used to different." Although He will never violate His written Word, one will almost always find Jesus in the "different." No matter how God speaks, we must be ready to listen, ready to receive.

Jesus never followed a prescribed pattern or allowed himself to be boxed in by some predetermined, prearranged method when He called people. Although He will never violate His written Word, you will almost always find Jesus in the "different." No matter how God speaks, we must be ready to listen, ready to receive.

Many people have given seminars or written books to provide the formula to hear God's voice, but we must understand that there is no one-size-fits-all methodology to achieve that purpose. Principles are important and biblical truths are priceless, but when we look at Scripture in its totality, we see that God has chosen many ways to speak to people. We can't simply bottle up a solution that works for everyone. God will never allow His guiding voice to be reduced to a methodology or prescription.

Whenever we think we've figured God out, He changes His action patterns.

I encourage you to think about what you'd do for God if life hadn't managed to get in the way. Maybe you've put off what God has placed in your heart because your responsibilities are too great. You can't even begin to fathom taking risks for God.

I encourage you to have a conversation with God about your fears, doubts, and struggles. Now is an excellent time to take a break from reading and journal your thoughts to God. No talking, no negotiating, just journaling. Pretend for a moment that life never unfolded for you the way it did. Pretend for a moment that you could start fresh. What would you attempt? To whom would you talk? What daring new life adventure would you undertake? Write it down. Don't think about whether it's realistic; just dream with your pen and see where it takes you. Different is God's way of speaking to those who are willing to listen. Are you ready to hear?

IT'S MICHELE'S TURN

*Beginnings are mysterious things, part breath, part
hope, part fumble, part grace. Roots are, historically,
perhaps the most humble of God's creations on earth.
They require neither acknowledgment nor praise. Their
reward is reaped when the living stand upon them
and reach for the fruit the roots made possible.[11]*

That girl from Camden, the girl that I met at the youth rally, became my wife. The desire God birthed in me as a young boy to marry a Puerto Rican wasn't some strange, off-the-wall inclination; it was real. God deposited this desire into me as a kid because He had a special girl waiting for me. I do believe God has a God-ordained mate, a God-ordained future family, a God-ordained future for us, but we can change that.

Think of Samson, who is found in the book of Judges. He was nothing short of a miracle, a man whose birth was a human impossibility. Samson's mother was barren and childless (Judges 13:2). This woman couldn't have children of her own. But God seems to love impossible stories because it demonstrates His God-authority. So, the angel of the Lord saw this barren woman and said:

> ...You are barren and childless, but you are going to become pregnant and give birth to a son. 4 Now see to it that you drink no wine or other fermented drink and that you do not eat anything unclean. 5 You will become pregnant and have a son whose head is never to be touched by a razor because the boy is to be a Nazarite, dedicated to God from the womb. He will take

the lead in delivering Israel from the hands of the Philistines (Judges 13).

Both the woman and her husband Manoah struggled to believe. At one point, they even thought they might die for having
experienced God (v. 23). Miraculously, the boy is born and raised
according to the conditions set forth by the angel of the Lord.

The essence of these first few chapters is wrapped up in verse
25, which tells us that the Spirit of the Lord began to "stir" him.
In other words, God himself was dropping what I call "natural
inclinations" into this miracle child. Samson didn't know it, but
God was working in him!

We must be very sensitive. We can't depend on having a climactic moment with God that rocks our world. Everyone's story
is different. Manoah and his wife had a climactic, transformational moment; for Samson, it began as a stirring from the
Spirit of God.

Individual Will

Has God been stirring you? Ask Him to help you to hear Him,
see Him, and help you connect with the Holy Spirit in a way
that opens your spiritual senses. You may not receive an immediate response from God, but what do you have to lose? If you
take every moment to still your spirit and listen to God, He will
speak to you. Like riding the bike or walking, you may not get it
right the first time; your ear may have to get fine-tuned. When
you have made yourself available, and God knows you're ready to
hear, the symphony will blow you away when the two join!

Unfortunately, the story of Samson doesn't end there. If you
read a little further into the narrative, you'll discover that Samson had a weakness for women. God called this man to deliver
Israel, yet he struggled with internal desires.

We can all relate. Whether you're a pastor, evangelist, or
prophet, we all struggle with human traits. You might even be
an incredible prayer warrior. You're still human and born with a
sinful nature that must be overcome daily, just like in Samson's

case. When Adam disobeyed God by eating the forbidden fruit, it opened the floodgates for every human to struggle with sin. Take a look at what Paul tells us in Romans 5:12-15:

> When Adam sinned, sin entered the world. Adam's sin brought death, so death spread to everyone, for everyone sinned. Yes, people sinned even before the law was given. But it was not counted as sin because there was not yet any law to break. Still, everyone died—from the time of Adam to the time of Moses—even those who did not disobey an explicit commandment of God, as Adam did. Now Adam is a symbol, a representation of Christ, who was yet to come. But there is a significant difference between Adam's sin and God's gracious gift. For the sin of this one man, Adam, brought death to many. But even greater is God's wonderful grace and his gift of forgiveness to many through this other man, Jesus Christ.

Except for Jesus, no one has ever lived a sinless life. And the truth of the matter is, we all struggle with sin and will continue this struggle until Jesus calls us home. That's why Paul says, "... be transformed by the renewing of your mind" (Rom. 12:2). Our minds and hearts are drawn to corrupting God's perfectness. There was only one solution to man's broken condition, a redeemer— a sinless sacrifice that could take away our sin. In the Old Testament, people sacrificed animals for the forgiveness of their sins. In the New Testament, Jesus showed up and said that if you accept and believe in His sacrifice by responding in faith and obedience, He will save us. "...All who love me will do what I say. My Father will love them, and we will come and make our home with each of them" (John 14:23).

Sadly, Samson got caught up in his human desires. Even though God set him up for success from birth, Samson chose to walk another path, one that led him to a prison sentence. "... the Philistines captured him and gouged out his eyes. They took him to Gaza, where he was bound with bronze chains and forced to grind grain in the prison" (Judges 16:21). God would use him again, but Samson would sacrifice his life in the process.

Was that God's plan all along? Absolutely not! Remember, God can make provisions for a God-ordained future, but we have the ability to change that. God will never override our will; He wants us to accept and choose His will over our own.

Innocence

Michele told me from the beginning, "I can't date you if you're not a Christian." As we grew older, it was my turn. Before getting married, I said to her, "Don't marry me if you're not willing to become a missionary." I knew at the time God was drawing my heart to Cuba, and if she was going to be a part of my life, she needed to realize that the commitment to me meant a commitment to God's call for me. We really had no idea what it meant to be missionaries; we had no idea of the sacrifices. To be honest, we were naïve eighteen-year-olds who were much more immature than we realized. So, now it was Michele's turn to respond.

Michele almost immediately and innocently responded with, "Of course I'm willing to become a missionary!" When she said yes, she didn't understand what it would look like to be a foreign missionary away from family, in another country, relying on God, and so much more. Michele's story is not mine to tell, but she gave me her permission to share the next part.

My Mission Call / by Michele Pérez

So, it's true! The love of my life asked me to be his wife, but it came with the stipulation that he had this "missionary call." He wanted me to be aware of this before he asked for my hand in marriage. I was a seventeen-year-old girl who was deeply in love. I didn't think twice about being a missionary. I tucked that thought away, and we immediately began making wedding plans. We married the next year at the ripe old age of eighteen. We were babies and knew nothing about what this journey would look like. We bought our first home and began to play house. Becoming a missionary never crossed my mind during that first year.

It was a tough first year of marriage for me. After only ten months of being newlyweds, I lost my baby brother Marco to the streets of Philadelphia. He was only eighteen-years-old. His death hit our family hard, and I questioned many things during the months that followed.

Shortly after my brother's death, Bob began to feel the burden of his call again. We talked about applying to become missionaries. However, the timing didn't feel right. My older sister Lucy lived in Rhode Island. If we left to become missionaries then, my mom would be left alone. I told Bob I wasn't ready yet. I remember him being so patient with me. He let me know that he'd wait until I felt ready. I remember thinking, "I may never be ready."

I became pregnant with our first daughter Priscilla shortly after my brother's death. At the time, our home church announced an upcoming mission trip to Argentina. Bob became excited about the possibility of us going. I came up with reasons why this trip was a bad idea. I'd be seven months pregnant then, and the crew would be doing construction work. There was no reason for me to go, plus money was also tight. It didn't make sense to me. He persisted and asked me to pray about it. Deep down in my heart, I had a feeling that this mission trip would reignite His call. I didn't want to be set up!

Bob came home from work one day and said, "Babe, if God miraculously provides the money for the trip and the doctor says you can fly, will you consider going?" I agreed to think about it and thought there was no way those two things would happen. So Michele-of-little-faith agreed to go if those two things happened.

One month before the trip money was due, someone came up and asked us, "I feel like you both need to be on this trip." The person wrote a check, and we walked out of the church in shock. The first condition was met. There was still one more hurdle: getting the approval of my doctor to fly. Being seven months pregnant, I was confident my doctor wouldn't let me fly.

At my next visit, we sat with the doctor and asked whether I should fly to another country. I remember her words exactly. She said, "Michele, you've been completely healthy your entire pregnancy. I don't see any reason why you shouldn't go." She reminded me to stay well-hydrated and not participate in any of the construction work.

I sat there in shock as my hubby smiled from ear to ear on the ride home. I sensed a feeling deep down inside that something big was going to happen on this trip, and to be honest, it scared me.

The day came to board the plane, and we were off. When we arrived in Argentina, our host missionary, Rocco Ditrolio, greeted us and took us to the site where the team would be doing the construction work. We pulled up to a large yellow-and-white tent. Folding chairs were set up on dirt floors. The team would work behind the tent for the next ten days. For the first three days, the team mixed cement and laid brick. I sat around feeling useless as I really couldn't help in any way except handing out water bottles. I spoke with an Argentine woman who I later found out worked with the youth. I found it easy to talk with her and ended up sharing my full testimony with her. She asked if I'd be willing to share my testimony with the youth that evening. The thought terrified me. I didn't want to do it because my Spanish was horrible. I began to make excuses. She replied, "I truly believe God wants to bless someone through your story."

When we got back to the hotel, I talked it over with Bob. He had been asked to preach at the evening crusades. God let me know that He was definitely on the move. That evening I took my first leap of faith, and the Lord used my broken Spanish to connect my story to many young girls. One girl, in particular, was destined to change my life forever.

Bob preached his little heart out in his broken Spanish, and they asked him to share again. We arrived early to that second service. I sat praying in the back, going back and forth arguing with the Lord. I prayed for Him to show me if missions was the path we were to take. I reminded the Lord that I had nothing to offer, had never been to Bible college, hated public speaking, and on and on. As I ended my prayer, I looked up and saw Alejandra (a girl from the youth group) walk in. She had come early to sweep the dirt floors. She took a broom from the corner and began to sweep the floor. I thought this was strange, but in some crazy way, it made the dirt look neat and tidy. As I watched her, I felt the Holy Spirit speak strongly into my heart. "What are you so afraid of? Why are you so selfish? Look at this young girl. I want to use your story to bless young women. Why don't you trust that I'll take care of your family?"

That was my biggest fear, and God knew it. I didn't want to leave my mom or the rest of my family because I genuinely thought that I was the one holding them together for so many years. At that moment, God reminded me that He was in control and would take care of my family. Alejandra had approached me after I spoke the night before with tears in her eyes. She had a similar story to mine, and I had prayed with her. She hugged me and said my story gave her hope to keep following Jesus. I'll never forget that moment for as long as I live. I've recalled that moment the last seventeen years of our missionary career to remind me that God not only called my husband, but He called me as well.

When we returned from Argentina, I called my sister, telling her we were going to submit our paperwork with the Assemblies of God World Missions. She said they were moving back to Jersey, and I began to cry. She asked me why I was crying. She had no idea that I had been asking the Lord to move her back closer to our mom. The Lord was already at work. I can genuinely say that this has been the most fantastic journey, and while it hasn't been easy, it has been worth it!

OUR FIRST GO AT MINISTRY

Live each day fully dedicated to the great cause
that gives your life meaning and purpose. Be
passionate and focused. Live each day dedicated to
bettering yourself, becoming stronger, wiser, more
knowledgeable, and deeper in character. Always
view your life as a work in progress. Keep reading,
learning, experiencing, growing, and improving.[12]

Praise God! Michele was finally on board, we were ready to begin ministry, but God still had many lessons for us to learn. We thought Cuba would be our first and final destination, but that wouldn't happen for quite some time—if it were to happen at all.

For a long time, I felt like God wanted me to write a book. I knew it should be about our story and our missions journey, but I didn't know what the book would look like. I had played with titles for months, trying to flesh out my book. Then one day I was on my way to a missions service in North Jersey when God spoke! Michele was driving as I worked in the car. We were both hoping the snow wouldn't make us late for the service. And then it happened, God spoke.

Remember, we were on the highway, it was snowing, Michele was there, and the radio was on. Amidst all of the chaos of the moment, I looked up and saw a flashing sign that said, "Delays ahead: Be prepared to stop."

That was the moment God spoke, and I was ready to listen. He used a simple road sign to project His voice. You see, part of hearing God speak has to do with constantly holding a conversation between you and the Holy Spirit.

Prayer is not something that simply happens in the early morning hours. Prayer should be a constant in our lives. We can learn to go about our day, keeping in constant communication with the Lord. They might be small conversations with God in our heads, times of worship, reading, or meditating. You can change a baby's diaper and still communicate with God. So, when I saw that sign, there was a deposit in my spirit that was unexplainable yet recognizable. I sensed in my spirit an invisible thumbs up from God. I immediately realized God was giving me the title through a simple road sign I'd have missed it if I hadn't been sensitive to God's voice. Hearing God is about being sensitive enough to know when God is trying to speak or guide. If having trouble listening or hearing, I often intentionally seek out wise counsel from individuals who have learned the art of hearing from God.

As an example, look at Samuel, the prophet of the Old Testament. He was just a boy when he first heard God. In 1 Samuel 3:4-5, we are told that that "...the Lord called Samuel," and Samuel answered, "I am here!" He ran to Eli and said, "I am here. You called me." Samuel was just a boy who had no experience hearing God's voice. Samuel would develop that trait over time.

Samuel, unable to distinguish the voice, runs to Eli again and says, "You called me?" Eli is puzzled. "No, I haven't said anything." Why couldn't Samuel recognize the voice as the Lord? "Samuel didn't yet know the Lord, and the Lord had not spoken directly to him yet" (1 Samuel 3:7). In other words, the biblical narrative teaches that hearing God is not always automatic; it can happen in phases. Within those phases are levels of clarity.

Three times Samuel heard God, yet each time he thought it was Eli. It's interesting to note that it wasn't until the third time that the prophet Eli finally got the message that it was God speaking to young Samuel. He said, "Look Samuel, the next time you hear that voice, say 'Speak, Lord. I am your servant, and I am listening.'" And when he did that, the Lord made His message clear to Samuel.

Maybe this is you? God may have tried speaking through highway billboards, TV shows, or church messages preached on Sunday mornings. But you haven't been able to connect the dots because you don't know how to listen and respond. You can know that God will use every tool available to Him, and nothing is off-limits. Over the next few days, practice talking to God throughout the day. And then shut your mouth and stay quiet long enough to listen. Ask questions to those around you who are both grounded and experienced in their faith. Before you know it, you might be driving down a highway when a blinking sign blurts out God's message to you.

At the end of the day, life is full of lessons—some hard, others easy. You never live the Christian life or experience the walk of faith without learning God-ordained lessons. Samuel's story was intentionally written to teach us something. God doesn't operate in the world of chance, and the Bible clearly shows that we must learn to hear God. I wish we could avoid some lessons, but unfortunately, that's not always how God trains us. My first encounter of really hearing God's inaudible voice took place in Blackwood, but that was only the start.

I knew if God called me to be a missionary, I needed to get involved in some sort of ministry. In the beginning, I wasn't sure where I fit in within the church system. If God were to use me as a missionary, I'd have to use what I had: limited Spanish and a limited formal theological education, but enormous zeal. Purchasing an amplifier and fifteen-inch subwoofers, I became a street preacher in Camden, New Jersey. I became an overnight entrepreneur missionary before I ever had any formal ministry training. Every Saturday, I hauled my equipment to the worst part of downtown Camden to set up and preach the Word in English and Spanish.

Education and mentorship are valuable, but sometimes the deep end is the best teacher. The corner became my pulpit. I preached amid drug transactions and even in the middle of people getting pounced on during fistfights. The places where no one else wanted to go were the places that excited me. Eventually, I learned of a church plant in Camden that needed help. Although I never sensed God pulling me in that direction, I felt I could serve the Lord well in that church. Michele and I were about twenty-one years old, we had our first daughter, and we wanted to minister for God. At that church, we soon served as both worship leaders and youth pastors. There were only around four white people in the congregation, including me, but I never saw myself as different.

All that mattered to me was that we were on assignment! The truth is that we all need to be on assignment—at all times. God doesn't expect all of us to be on full-time clergy appointments, but He expects us to be "on assignment."

My good friend and mentor Don Cartledge, a missionary for the Assemblies of God, recently preached a fantastic message from Nehemiah about "Staying on the Wall." The Jewsish people of that day knew having a fortified wall that protected the city was vital to survival against enemies. But sadly, they let their wall crumble and were left unprotected. The wall failed its intended purpose. God recruited Nehemiah to help the people understand that they needed protection. Nehemiah convinced them they could and should have a wall. He helped them see that every person needed to play a role in getting that wall back to its God-designed purpose.

Here's a twist to this story. Jesus taught that He came to institute a new kingdom, the Kingdom of heaven. "The main thrust of the Kingdom is the spiritual transformation of persons who together form the body of Christ... The Kingdom is already present, but not yet complete. It is both present and future."[13] I think Jesus imagined there would also be a wall around this heavenly kingdom; however, this wouldn't be a concrete wall. It was to be a wall consisting of a multitude of people fulfilling their God-assignments. You and I personify this wall. God gifted us as prophets, teachers, pastors, prayer intercessors, missionaries, the Holy Spirit, His written Word, and so much more. Why? Because when you and I, as followers of Christ, are gifted in these areas, we replace the concrete material once used to fortify these earthly kingdoms. We each have assignments to perform within this kingdom, and these assignments lead to the protection and growth of this one-of-a-kind God-kingdom.

Recently, the Kingdom of God lost a dear soldier by the name of Mark Bose. As an independent missionary in India, Mark chased a passion that the Lord put in his heart many years ago. This passion was for the people of India to know Jesus, to experience this kingdom. Sadly, Mark was among the many infected by the outbreak of COVID in that country. After a long-fought battle for his health, Mark went home to be with Jesus. I honestly can't imagine the anguish his family experienced at his passing. I'm sure they wrestled with many questions about why God allowed COVID to take Mark's life. Mark clearly understood the parable of the ten servants in Luke 19. Jesus tells of a man of noble birth who entrusted his money to ten servants and said, "Occupy till I come" (KJV Luke 19:13). In modern-day terminology, the master expected these servants to be wise investors who actively worked to provide him with a return on his investment. The nobleman returned to discover that because of fear, one of his servants squandered the opportunity. He took back the money from the servant while he blessed the others. Jesus's purpose in telling the story was to teach us that He calls us to be active kingdom builders. He not only expects us to replace the concrete walls of earthly kingdoms but also to actively advance the Kingdom of God by jointly using our gifts.

Jesus knew there would be attacks on this divine kingdom. While He encouraged us to count the cost (Luke 14:25-35), Jesus never hesitated in inviting us to join in his mission to seek and save the lost. Mark Bose responded because Jesus called him. Today, he is with Jesus. Now, who will fill his shoes? Many will never know the name Mark Bose, but Jesus knows him. There are Indians who will one day be in heaven because of a missionary named Mark Bose. Jesus knows the pain of Mark's wife, Julie Bose. I honestly believe Jesus grieved with Mark's two daughters thousands of miles away from their native home in the United States. Mark sacrificed himself for the Kingdom of God because he believed he played a vital role in doing what the nobleman asked of his servants, "Occupy till I come." Mark recognized Jesus called him to be an active kingdom builder.

Nehemiah recognized there were threats all around that could destroy the work of rebuilding the wall. Still, he determined to return the people to their labors. He knew a strong wall and a strong kingdom depended on people actively participating and using their giftings to the best of their ability. These kinds of people are "active kingdom builders," fulfilling their "God-assignment." Paul discussed this message in the New Testament:

> After all, who is Apollos? Who is Paul? We are only God's servants through whom you believed the Good News. Each of us did the work the Lord gave us...we are both God's workers. And you are God's field. You are God's building (1 Corinthians 3:5-9).

When I said yes to the church in Camden, it wasn't because I thought I was God's gift to humanity; it was because I knew I had an assignment to fulfill. I knew I could play a role in building the wall that surrounds and protects the Kingdom of God. Like my buddy Don said, "Nehemiah worked the people harder than a borrowed mule." In other words, we need to be on assignment, staying active as members of this kingdom, using our gifts. Don's words were an excellent description of our work in the Camden church.

Michele and I were trying to follow God and give Him every opportunity to speak to us and use us. The learning curve was steep. It was our first time in ministry in a formal setting, but we were committed. Sometimes, it's easy to associate serving God with nothing else but blessings, joy, happiness, and so forth, but then reality sets in. Life doesn't always turn out the way we expect. Life is full of obstacles, challenges, and hurdles. Yes, there are moments of blessings, joy, and happiness, but when you consider the whole counsel of the Word of God, you find that life is hard. Real life is full of both the good and the bad.

I was a young man, young in my faith and not very jaded by life when I started in Camden. If I were to describe myself accurately with one word, it would have to be naïve. Life can be a cruel teacher, but you are more prone to take risks when you have not had those life-shattering lessons, trusting God to do greater things. Life may have played out quite differently had God given me a better picture as to what our future would hold. In other words, one can also see naivety as a gift.

When we started at the Camden church, we were young parents. I knew we'd need help with the ministry, so we reached out to key individuals who could help. One person was the lead pastor's daughter. We were friends since we were teenagers. I soon learned running family churches with immediate family in leadership positions was dangerous territory. Friendships aside, even family-run businesses have the same challenges. Anything that's family-run has the potential of becoming toxic to outsiders who are not part of the family. This experience proved to be a painful life lesson.

Like so many other life lessons, I had to live the experience first-hand to learn it as a life lesson. Michele and I started working with the pastor's daughter, and in the beginning, things went well. Be aware that it's almost always that way—until the bomb drops, whether in one month, one year, or even ten years. Things were going well until they weren't.

Please let me share another vital leadership lesson I learned in the trenches. Always keep your mission, goals, vision for life, and ministry crystal clear and in front of you at all times. If you're a leader, your organization, church, or wherever you lead needs to know about these unwritten driving forces. If you're a follower (and there's nothing wrong in following the right people), make sure your personal mission aligns well with the mission of your church or organization. People, life, and even circumstances have a way of taking you off track. You may drift so far in the current of life that you forget who you are and what God has called you to do.

Our friend, the pastor's daughter, ultimately disagreed with the direction we were taking the youth. She felt youth work should be done differently. She took her disagreement to her dad, the pastor. He later asked us to meet with him. We sat down to discuss the situation at hand, and he said he felt God wanted us to take a step back from leading the youth. This news was a shock. Never the quickest at responding in a confrontation, I tried to process his words quickly. Caught off guard, I measured my response.

Although my spirit felt attacked, I said, "Well, you know what, I'm okay with that. Things have been tense, and I've been thinking of taking a step back. But I feel if we do, we could focus more on creating a better worship experience. And I love leading worship."

Now you'd think that the conversation would have ended there, but that's when the bomb dropped.

This pastor listened to what we said, but his response changed everything. As I sat there comfortable with my reply, he said, "Well, hearing this, I feel like not only should you step back from the youth, but I'm also going to ask you to step down from the worship team."

He completely blindsided me. If the first put-down didn't sting enough, the second walloped us. He initially used God as the excuse for his demand, but when God wasn't enough of a reason, the pastor found a way to somehow crush our spirits. The wound was so severe that I considered giving up on church, ministry, and ever serving God again. Self-pity overtook my spirit. All I wanted to do was serve God, yet God allowed something like this to happen. I couldn't believe it.

I was at a breaking point. Young, naïve, and green in the ministry, my first hurdle almost destroyed me. Other people distracted me, even if for a brief moment, from my God-assignment. This is life. If you're not careful, people, life, and even circumstances can carry you away from your mission, goals, and life vision.

But God sent other people who were fulfilling their God-given assignments my way to get me back on mission. I reached out to my childhood pastor and told him where I was in my faith. I felt demoralized and knocked down, just like Nehemiah's wall! The funny thing is that God waited until I was at my lowest point before He spoke through my pastor. When I told him I wanted to quit on God, the pastor didn't say, "I'm sorry Bob," or "That's so hard to hear." He said, "Bob, if you think that's bad, you should be ashamed of yourself because ministry gets worse." Ouch.

God spoke to me even if it was something I didn't want to hear. God spoke through a pastor who understood his role as an active kingdom builder. He was fulfilling his God-given assignment. Thank God, this pastor both protected the kingdom and encouraged me as a believer. I didn't need to be coddled. I needed hard words that would shake me. Others may have been offended, and some may have cursed that pastor for his harshness, but young Bob needed tough love.

I could have easily missed God speaking that day, but twenty-three years later, I remember those words vividly, and I still see their relevance. Not only is life hard, but so is ministry. Those words got me back to my God-assignment; it got me back to my labors. Yes, those words slowed me down. There were delays, but I needed those delays. Here's what I learned: sometimes when you're following God, delays will happen, and you need to be prepared to stop.

Pastor Kurt Kinney (Bethel Church, Blackwood), thank you! Thank you for letting God use you to speak to me that day. Thank you for living as an active kingdom builder who walks in step with their God-assignment as a pastor. If you had not been there that day when I considered quitting on God, who knows if missionary Bob would have ever materialized. You were just one piece of the puzzle in my God-journey, but you were an eternally important piece.

WAVES OF REJECTION

*You guide me with your counsel, leading me
to a glorious destiny. Psalm 73:24*

Now what? I asked myself. I just had a moment with God through a meeting with my childhood pastor. I thought, *Where do I go? What do I do? Should I be discouraged? Should I be excited? Or do I go back into what was a toxic situation?*

Many of you may struggle with these same questions. The truth is that the answer won't stare you in the face. You may have anxiety or doubt about what to do, but that's normal. Welcome to the human race. God's Word says, "If any of you lacks wisdom, you should ask God, who gives generously to all without finding fault, and it will be given to you" (James 1:5). This verse is the first part of our response: ask God those questions I just posed to you. Matthew 7:7-8 says, "Ask, and it will be given to you; seek, and you will find; knock, and the door will be opened to you. For everyone who asks receives; the one who seeks finds; and to the one who knocks, the door will be opened." Part of our response to those situations must revolve around asking God for wisdom. Yet, there's also an implicit part two.

We have to do something. We have to move. God told us in His Word that He would give us wisdom; however, He never said how soon. That's the challenging part of following God. God's timetables are not our timetables. So often, I've wished for the map of life that would show us the steps from A to Z. I've gone so far as praying for those maps with great urgency. I am now forty-three years old, and God has yet to answer that prayer. I doubt He ever will. Imagine if I did have the map. Why would there be the necessity to depend on God?

Think about Elijah in 1 Kings 19. Elijah was following God when faced with a moment where he killed all of Ahab's prophets. Then Ahab's wife, Jezebel, sent a message to Elijah that said, "May the gods deal with me, and ever so severely, if by this time tomorrow I do not make your life like the lives of those you killed!" Elijah panicked, crying out to the Lord, "I have had enough, Lord, take my life, for I am no better than my fathers." He didn't know God's A-to-Z plan. If Elijah had known the consequences of his actions, he might have never done what he did. God knows this. He knows we must be kept in ignorance at times if we're going to follow through with what He wants us to do.

You might think God would have been mad at Elijah's fear. He may have chuckled in heaven, "If Elijah only knew My plan." I don't know why so many believe God gets mad when we struggle with our walk of faith, but that's not true. The Bible is full of examples of people of God who struggled with fear, faith, or simply getting the courage to follow him. There's no sin in those human traits—it's at its essential core, human.

Now, if we stay stuck in our misery instead of moving, that's another story. Staying stuck shows dependence on oneself, but moving means dependence on God, even when we don't understand or see the entire map. A Chilean friend texted me, writing, "I read your recent sermon excerpt about following God, and you said to jump into the deep end. Why not say, follow God to the mountaintop? Don't you think that would sound better?" My reply was immediate. I said, "Cristián, if I jump in the deep end, I cut off all bridges back to where I started. Provided I don't know how to swim, God has to act immediately, or I die. Whereas if I follow God to the mountaintop, there's the possibility that I get there thinking I did it on my power, strength, or ingenuity." There will never be anything wrong with the fear of getting in the deep end. God isn't afraid of our fear, but He expects us to refrain from being paralyzed in response to life. We have to move.

Elijah wanted to die, but still, the angel of the Lord touched him and said, "Get up and eat" (1 Kings 19:5), and then he left. The Bible says the angel came back a second time with the same command and said, "Get up and eat, or the journey will be too much for you" (v. 7), Elijah ate, drank, was strengthened, and then set out on a journey that lasted "forty days and forty nights until he reached Horeb, the mountain of God" (v. 8). The Lord didn't say anything about the journey taking forty days of walking. Elijah had to have been hungry, even parched, yet he marched on—not knowing—until one day he reached the mountain. "And the word of the Lord came to him" (v. 9).

If there's one method recorded that God routinely uses in the Bible, it's the art of the controlled voice. He waits, waits, and then waits some more until the right time; in His time, He speaks. However, if we do fail to act, this controlled voice may never come. God can speak in our stagnation, but the overwhelming majority of Scripture indicates that movement produces a God response.

I don't advocate jumping at every opportunity only for the sake of movement. We need to move slowly, seeking God's wisdom, and spend time with God in prayer and His Word. However, there will come a point where you must act and move. This process is different for everyone. Unfortunately, there's no boxed answer to the question of when it will happen for you. But, if you follow Jesus close enough, you'll learn to sense God-proddings, God-nudges.

In my case, my childhood pastor had just given me a stern word, and that God-word required a response. It wasn't a good choice to return to the toxic environment in Camden. Bethel Church wasn't the right place for me either because it was too comfortable. I needed to spread my wings and fly. You may not walk on your first step or ride that bike on the very first try, but it doesn't make you a failure. I honestly didn't know what to do. I did the next best thing. I left the Camden church and began to attend a faith-filled, Bible-believing preaching church in Pennsauken. This is where I waited for our next instruction from God.

Some of you might be in toxic situations as I was. The Camden pastor had demoralized me to the point that I was ready to give up on God. I couldn't get over how he tried to use God in his efforts to control me. Are people using God, trying to control you? Stop and think about what you're going through. Maybe you never recognized that fact until this moment. Here's wisdom if you want to get out of your situation:

(1) Join a local church that preaches the Word of God
(2) Get God's unadulterated Word in you, read with no external help
(3) Surround yourself with experienced, mature people of faith with whom you can ask questions
(4) Involve yourself in a small group community of believers who walk out their faith together.

I wear a pastor hat as one of my many duties, and I know that no one gets it right all of the time. Love your pastor, respect your pastor, pray for your pastor, but ultimately know, the Lord is your shepherd. Pastors have some of the most challenging jobs. Between dealing with the church, people's issues, life-shattering events, and church funding, pastors are incredible heroes of the faith. We need your prayers and your support more than you know. However, pastors are still humans with flaws and problems. Our job is to watch the flock, but that doesn't mean we will never make mistakes. When King Solomon penned Proverbs 15:22, he spoke to pastors, ministers, parents, kids, and every human who would walk the face of the earth. While he didn't say that we're all capable of flaws and problems, he left us with a simple practice that would put each of us on a path to making good decisions. He said, "Plans go wrong for lack of advice; many advisers bring success." Thank God for the body of Christ and the multitude of counselors.

While attending the Pennsauken church, Michele and I talked over the issues. Maybe it was time for us to pursue a missionary appointment with the Assemblies of God. We made our decision, knowing the group is a great denomination with healthy biblical doctrine and a strong emphasis on missions.

When we first arrived at the Pennsauken church, I sat down with the pastor and explained what happened in the Camden Assemblies of God church. For one reason or another, the Camden church drifted from their original DNA and broke free from the oversight of the Assemblies of God. We discussed the church, my role, and all that had taken place. I confessed, "Pastor Dan, I want to be a missionary. I feel like this is a healthy home for now, but I want you to know, this is my goal. I'm currently working as a full-time senior network engineer, a job that I love, but I can't escape the fact that God has called me to be a missionary. I came so close to giving up on God after what happened in Camden, but I recognize I need to be an active kingdom builder. I'm running my race again, and if it's okay with you, I'd like for Calvary Pennsauken to be my home church in the meantime." After a hug from the pastor and a warm welcome, Calvary became our home. We may not live in New Jersey anymore, but Calvary Pennsauken is still our home because of great people and a great pastor, and for being a church that believes in one word, God's Word.

God never visibly directed us to Pennsauken, although I wish He would have said something. God was silent on the whole issue. Or was He? I sought God and had many conversations with other people. Even though God seemed silent, I wondered if He guided our conversation with Pastor Dan. As I shared our ministry story and we sought God together, a special relationship was built—a friendship that endures to this day. I believe God was there, silently guiding us. He has continued to guide us every day in ways that would eventually lead me to write our story.

Pastor Dan supported our decision to apply for the missionary appointment. As my pastor, he was instrumental in requesting a meeting before the New Jersey district of the Assemblies of God. I didn't know that Pastor Dan was a big missions supporter and very close to all of the New Jersey missions team members. I didn't strategically pursue specific individuals to achieve my God vision; yet, God always positioned me wherever I needed to be to get the instruction, training, and life lessons necessary for the next step.

With the help of Pastor Dan, my application soon hit the desk of the New Jersey Assemblies of God Missions Task Force, which meant more meetings and conversations. Conversations are meaningful, but it felt as if we were wasting precious time. I thought, *God, pick up the pace already!* If you identify with me, I can guarantee this: your faith walk will become very frustrated. God is timely, and He has His own timetable. His timing looks nothing like ours. It can be frustrating at times.

So here we were in Trenton, meeting with the Missions Committee. One man asked very pointed questions. "How much are you willing to sacrifice?" Little did we know he was a missionary with considerable wisdom and experience. I guess he understood what Phillip Yancey meant when he said, "Faith means believing in advance what will only make sense in reverse." This brother experienced what it meant to live by faith. He probably had those moments that didn't make any sense until he got to the other side and could understand. By posing that question, he wanted to know if I was ready for that faith commitment, especially when things looked impossible. I haven't seen him since that interview, but Brother, that was a great question to contemplate.

Somehow, by God's grace, we got through the meeting. I was told, "Now, you'll have to wait." There was no time frame, no ETA, just wait. And wait, we did.

Experiencing Cycles of Growth

After a few weeks, still excited about our potential future in missions, I finally got the expected phone call. The missions task force received the response they were waiting on from the Assemblies of God headquarters. I had a smile on my face and felt excitement building in my heart until the missions director Rich Leksell said, "Bob, there's a problem. You have some debt. Unfortunately, one of the requirements for missionary applicants seeking appointment is no debt."

At that moment, I almost dropped the phone in despair. "No, this can't be," I screamed inside. But it was. That was the Assemblies of God policy. There was nothing to do other than to somehow get out of debt. Not the best at handling money when I was younger, it was a problem I had created.

Kids think they can get everything right away that their parents worked forty years to buy. This problem suddenly gave me an epiphany. I needed to sell our house. Michele and I bought our first house when I was eighteen years old. It was one of those houses that needed a lot of work, which meant I financed some of the materials. I did most of the work myself, but the materials were financially beyond my reach as we renovated the place. We listed the house, and almost miraculously, we received a full-price offer overnight.

God didn't offer audible solutions, but I knew He had called me when I was a boy. We needed to do something if we were going to be missionaries. Who needs a house anyway, right? Be cautious in making rash decisions like selling your house to serve God. But for me at this time, I knew God was in this. That meant doing what was necessary, even if we had to make sacrifices. Where were we going to live? Thanks, Mom and Dad for taking us in. We moved back home with my parents, hoping that the process wouldn't be too long. These were faith moves, moves that often don't have clear roadmaps.

Rich Leksell re-sent my application to the Assemblies of God World Missions. They called a few weeks later to ask if it was true that Michele was now pregnant with our second child. Yes, it was true. They told Rich, "Brother, for the appointment they are seeking, the policy states they can only have one child." First, I was rejected because of debt, so I sold my house, moved in with my mom and dad, and now they were going to reject me because of a pregnancy? Yes, sir, that's right. Rich, too, was even shocked at the news. I learned later that he said, "If you're going to turn them down because of this kid, I'm not going to tell them. You have to do it." He could only do so much because these decisions are made at the national office, but I was glad to have him in my corner. Fortunately, the Assemblies of God overlooked the child issue and later called to ask that Michele and I meet with their family life director at the Philadelphia airport. We were finally moving forward. The sun was finally shining.

Fast forward a few months, and I had the most significant interview of my lifetime. After all the delays I experienced along the way, the Assemblies of God was finally 'dandome pelota' (giving me an opportunity). I was succeeding in life, but there was never a question in my mind that God called me to missions and the country of Cuba. I was actively involved in my wonderful home church. I was working as a senior network engineer at a fantastic secular start-up dot-com business in Delaware. I had a beautiful office, an excellent salary, and life was just easy. Life was working out for me in every way. I was well-respected at my job and doing what I wanted and loved to do. Being responsible for the company's cybersecurity was outstanding. I traveled to Arizona, to offices in San Francisco, and my role within the company was great except for being on call twenty-four hours a day, seven days a week. When I stepped into that meeting at the airport, it was not because I could not pursue other viable avenues to have a good, life-long career. I was a successful engineer, we now had a great family of four since Isabella's birth, and if you were to look at our lives from the outside, we checked all the boxes of what it meant to be successful. However, I had to pursue the reason God created me, which went beyond computers.

Things went downhill quickly after the interview started. Working with code in front of a computer screen all day, I wasn't the most astute at reading people. I was an engineer. My interviewer gave no facial cues as to what he was thinking; however, I somehow knew things weren't going as they should, at least concerning myself. As we left that day, I felt that Michele had knocked the interview out of the park. She did a phenomenal job and had all the qualities of a missionary. In contrast, it seemed I was the exact opposite of what they wanted. But maybe I read the situation all wrong. I had already been forced to overcome a few significant hurdles just getting to the interview. Even though I walked away feeling like I bombed the interview, I was still optimistic about the outcome. I totally trusted God. I quoted Romans 8:28 where Paul says, "And we know that all things work together for good to them that love God, to them who are the called according to his purpose." How could things not work out this time?

One, two, then three months passed by, but we heard nothing. No calls, no emails, nothing. I called Rich to inquire, and he said he'd get back to us. When he finally phoned back, he informed me that the Assemblies of God would call me later that evening. As Michele and I sat down for dinner that evening, we received that phone call.

"Bob, you're just not ready yet. We think you need to get more pastoral experience under your belt. Why don't you give it another year and then reach out to us... Goodbye." At this point, it got real. Did I really trust God? Did I trust that my childhood call was real? I hung up the phone and went silent. With my heart in my throat, I tried eating my dinner. My wife and I didn't exchange many words until I dropped my fork, spit out the beans, and started to weep.

These were challenging moments. It felt like God was constantly hanging me out to dry. Every time I turned around, something else seemed to go wrong. But it only seemed to go wrong when we talked about ministry. Could that be a clue I wasn't cut out for ministry? It was a possibility. But I also asked myself if God needed to drag me through some muddy moments to make sure I could endure what lay ahead for Michele and me? That was more likely to be the case. For me, these were what I would call my desert moments. God allowed himself to appear distant, uninterested, and even uninvolved. Mark Altrogge better describes these moments this way, "When we're in the desert, it can feel like God's not doing anything. Or he's set us aside. But God is always at work."[14]

I'd never want to compare my experiences with Jesus, but even He reached such a low point during the crucifixion that He said, "My God, my God, why have you abandoned me?" (Matthew 27:46). At that moment, when Jesus bore the sin of humanity, God the Father had to turn away. He left His Son alone on the cross, surrounded by haters. David, the man after God's own heart, cried out, "My God, my God, why have you abandoned me? Why are you so far away when I groan for help?" (Psalm 22:1). In my way, I felt like God did the same with me. He left me to fend for myself. I was already hurt by a pastor, rejected because of debt, almost rejected because of a pregnancy, and now this. "Wait another year."

I didn't know what to do with this answer, so rather than turn away discouraged, I chose to focus on the words, "Come back in another year."

We all choose what words we hear and what we keep in our hearts. Think about the story of the father who tells his two sons that they're failures. One son internalizes the message negatively. Maybe he goes down the addiction road, allowing addictions to destroy his life simply because he can't get away from those hurtful words. Then, there's the other son who hears those exact words and says, "A failure, huh? I'll show you! There's no way I'll fail." And that son turns out to be a great business success. One kid, defeated; the other, an overcomer. Whichever side of the equation you find yourself on can be traced back to how you received those words. My story could've turned out differently had I heard, "You're not ready." But I chose to hear, "Come back in another year." I realized we had to do something. We had to keep moving.

I met with Pastor Dan and said, "Pastor, I need your help. The Assemblies of God said to give it another year. They said I needed to develop more pastoral and people skills." My pastor was an Italian from the Bronx. He was a hugger and a very charismatic pastor who understood emotional IQ from his upbringing.

These were the very characteristics that "engineer Bob" lacked. What made me excel at my job as a network engineer turned out to be a deficit for ministry. We came up with a plan to help me, which would go on for the next year. He taught me how to smile —not that I couldn't smile, but it wasn't a natural response for me. In pictures, I was Mr. Serious. I said "Hi" to people with a New Jersey head nod. I found it somewhat intimidating to say hi or engage people in conversations. I could do it, but I had to work at it.

At church, Pastor Dan and other people worked to soften my engineer mannerisms into a more approachable and friendlier appearance. When there would be opportunities for photoshoots at church, Pastor Dan stood in the background saying, "Show those teeth, smile." And I did. I started leading small groups so that I'd be forced to interact with people. Spies were put on alert to keep an eye on me and report if I didn't say hi. I forced myself into a growth cycle where accountability was all around me. We structured an environment that would give me the best chance to develop the skills I needed when we reapplied. Not only had we worked hard at our local church level, but we also participated in a Spanish church plant some ten miles away in Blackwood with my friend, Brother Joe Vélez, along our one-year road. More about that in chapter 8.

Ultimately, one year later, my application was back in again. A short time later, we heard that we were being officially considered as missionary candidates. We weren't entirely accepted yet as our acceptance depended on our interview that would take place in Springfield, Missouri, in October of that year.

I thought I was going to make many sacrifices along the missionary journey. And yes, that was true. However, I wasn't the only one. When I started my application, I ended up living with Mom and Dad. When I decided to join missions, my parents also had to say yes to missions and make sacrifices. Thanks, Mom and Dad for your amazing support over the many years. I honestly don't deserve all that you have done for me. Still, you both have chosen to make your sacrifices alongside Michele and me.

Furthermore, realize that your decisions don't only affect you! All of our choices affect those around us in some way or another. My parents, my wife, my kids, those around us have made many sacrifices as well. And remember, if you make the right decisions, wait on God, and endure waves of rejection, just maybe, "Today will be the best day of your life, and tomorrow will be even better," as Zig Ziglar said.

MISSIONS ORIENTATION

Samuel examines the boys one at a time like canines on leashes, more than once ready to give the blue ribbon, but each time God stops him.[15]

God does not see the same way people see. People look on the outside of a person, but the Lord looks at the heart. 1 Samuel 16:7 NCV

October arrived. Missionary candidate orientation would soon be in full swing. The only way we could attend orientation was without the kids. Mom and Dad committed and sacrificed their time to watch them. Michele and I spent two weeks at the Assemblies of God headquarters in Missouri with the other missionary candidates from every walk of life, all seeking appointments. Most came from some pastorate, whereas others had a trade skill they planned to use on the mission field. That was kind of my story. I was currently working full-time as a network engineer and doing my part at a local church. I had no immediate family in the ministry. In fact, the majority of my family came from blue-collar jobs in the automotive world. I grew up around cars all my life.

So here were Bob and Michele in Missouri seeking missionary appointments at the Assemblies of God headquarters, surrounded by professional church people. I felt like a fish out of water. I hadn't even let my employer know that I was applying to be a missionary. Being employed at a bank as a senior network engineer meant I had access to thousands of credit cards. If my employer knew I was seeking another job, they might have terminated my contract. I kept the whole missionary application top-secret for months. It was probably one of the best-kept secrets I've ever had to hold for so long. The dream was finally becoming a reality. I had experienced so many waves of rejection that I honestly couldn't believe this was all happening. It was surreal but awesome.

The two-week orientation had a purpose. All missionary candidates had to meet with the executive committee to make their case for ministry. We sat at a huge table surrounded by area directors, executive leaders, and the director of the Assemblies of God World Missions at that time, Reverend John Bueno. These were days of many teachings. We had to sit through many lectures, which had the intention of helping us download the DNA of the Assemblies of God. We were encouraged to build relationships. Many of the candidates at that event are still friends to this day, even though we're scattered across the globe. Over the past twenty years, some didn't continue in foreign missions, but they are still dear friends, and we keep in touch with them using social media.

Not one person has all of the answers in the Assemblies of God missions program. Like any organization, you'll always find people who think they have all the answers, but I thank God that our leaders have been chosen carefully through prayer. Part of the process is having "conversations." Leaders are selected as a result of many conversations. Similar to how companies like Microsoft, Apple, or Google won't ever appoint a CEO without a thorough investigation to determine his or her suitability for the job, the Assemblies of God won't consider appointing someone without thoroughly vetting him or her. The vetting process is quite extensive.

Every missionary candidate was given a thorough personality test, which measured many different aspects. Our peers, pastors, and circles of influence had to send multiple references and information to provide insight about us. In the past, the Assemblies of God would send a representative to candidates' houses. The representative then stayed with them for a few days to experience their home life. As an organization, they were and continue to be serious about a rigorous process that thoroughly vets candidates. It's unlikely that you'll haphazardly reach this point in the application process. Once you're in, the vetting doesn't stop.

The executive committee has great control over selecting or rejecting future missionaries and can stop missionaries dead in their tracks. I loved the fact that decisions were made using group conversations under the public lens of the committee. Once again, the committee asked missionaries to explain and, in some cases, defend their call. After this process, the committee prays and asks God for guidance in selecting those who will pass on for further consideration. More individualized conversations would follow to flesh out missionary candidates' roles and discuss the country where they might serve their appointment.

I was nervous. I didn't know what to expect. I knew nothing that I know now. Everything was new and unexpected. The interesting thing is that even up until this point, we had never talked about finances. I had no idea how salaries worked, how much I'd receive as a salary, or if I'd receive any sort of medical benefits. It wasn't part of the conversation.

Looking back, I might have thought that there would have been grounds to dismiss my application if I brought it up. But, from my perspective, I believed one needs to have both faith and trust in God. The call also helps you look beyond the money. If money is your driving force, as is the case in most careers, you might as well quit, hang up your gloves, and go home. There's nothing wrong with working for money. One of the things I loved about my computer job was the money. I had made strategic organizational changes in my career, first to advance my position and second to make more money. Yes, I did make more money. No one, including Jesus, ever said that to serve God, we had to be poor.

Scripture tells of a man who wanted to follow Jesus. Jesus told him to go home, sell everything, and then follow Him (Mark 10:21). That doesn't mean we should sell everything we own. Sometimes you must look beyond the biblical narrative to understand why Jesus did or said what He did. We know this man was rich (Luke 18:23), and he was a ruler (Luke 18:18). From all external measurements, he had the whole package to succeed in life. Jesus might have thought, *This man wants to inherit eternal life. I could make him a follower and grow My fame.* But true to Jesus's character, that's not His modus operandi. Instead, Jesus goes to the core of this man's heart. I have to believe this man's request to follow Jesus was genuine. He didn't show up in secret, nor did he choose to approach Jesus under cover of night. He stood before Jesus and bowed down as a sign of respect (Mark 10:17). But Jesus saw something unspoken in this man's heart He had to address publicly. Knowing the heart of this rich ruler, Jesus called him out. This man's inability to part with his wealth kept him from following in the footsteps of the Master. It wasn't that his wealth or position was the issue; it was his heart's connection with those things. While the man was seemingly earnest in his request, he still had his own conditions for following Jesus. These needed to be addressed and brought into the light. As the Matthew Henry Commentary says, "He was sad at that saying, was sorry that he couldn't be a follower of Christ upon any easier terms than leaving all to follow him...But since he couldn't come up to the terms of discipleship...He went away grieved."

How often does that narrative mirror our lives, but maybe in other areas of life? We think, *Lord, I'll follow you. Send me wherever you want me to go.* However, in the deep recesses of our hearts, we hold onto things that take precedence over God. Some of those things are so precious. Michele and I were in the process of applying as missionaries, which required us to make certain sacrifices, but our God-given purpose never exempted us from wrestling with internal sacrifices. God wants each one of us at some point to struggle with ourselves – to recognize things that honestly might pre-empt God. Try to follow Jesus, and you'll see what I mean.

Jeremiah, God's prophetic voice from the Old Testament, knew this before Jesus ever stepped onto the scene. He said, "The human heart is the most deceitful of all things, and desperately wicked. Who really knows how bad it is?" (Jeremiah 17:9). Paul, the apostle, openly confessed, "I don't really understand myself, for I want to do what is right, but I don't do it. Instead, I do what I hate" (Romans 7:15). Finally, read Jesus's final words, where He says,

> If any of you wants to be my follower, you must give up your own way, take up your cross, and follow me. If you try to hang on to your life, you will lose it. But if you give up your life for my sake, you will save it. And what do you benefit if you gain the whole world but lose your own soul? Is anything worth more than your soul? (Matthew 16:24-26).

God knows following Jesus will stretch us. That was always His intent!

My thoughts of trying to talk about salary or benefits during the missionary interview process might end in an application dismissal. The executives might interpret my questions as a condition for accepting a missions appointment. I'll tell you this: if, like the rich man, money is your heart struggle, missions may not be the place for you. Because as my area director Don Exley once told me, "Assemblies of God missionaries are faith missionaries." You'll most likely struggle financially at least once, if not many times in your career. This struggle will be different for everyone. You may never have this experience, but don't be surprised if you do. God doesn't just want you. He also wants your heart! I love the song "Refiner" by Maverick City. It goes like this:

> *I wanna be tried by fire*
> *Purified*
> *You take whatever You desire*
> *Lord, here's my life*

You, too, might be tempted to sing this song. Perhaps the worship team in your church sings it as a familiar melody. Perhaps as it leaves your lips, tears run down your cheeks. You may have your hands extended to heaven, knees on the ground in a position of total submission. These are all great forms of offering worship. We benefit from surrendering ourselves to God in this fashion. But friend, when you do so, do so carefully because God wants your heart! He knows the difference between heart worship and just-for-show worship. When you truly surrender, there's a good possibility that what initially started as a light commitment becomes a walk of intense faith and a walk of challenging obedience. Very few will ever experience this walk of life. But, in those times when you stop long enough to listen, you'll hear God.

The missions executive team asked us many questions, most of which I've forgotten, except for two. The first question was, "What will you do if your wife's ministry takes off and you have to stay home and take care of the kids?" To the best of my knowledge, I said, "If that's what God has in mind, I'll support my wife." You'll have to ask her if she thinks that has been the case. I tend to think I'd be biased in my answer. The second question was, "Which country?" *That's an easy one*, I thought. *Cuba*. God had taken me through so many rejections at that point. Other than my mom, grandpop, and pastor, very few people thought Cuba was possible. Still, I knew what God had dropped in my spirit as a young boy in Blackwood at Bethel Church. The World Missions director, John Bueno, responded by sharing some personal stories from his experience with that country. Soon after that, the committee explained to me that Cuba wasn't going to happen. They didn't give me all of the details; they just told me that Cuba wasn't possible. What I heard was, "Your dream is simply impossible." The door was slammed and shut tightly. Just when I tried to walk into my destiny, it was ripped away from me again. I didn't get turned down for a missionary appointment, only turned down with regard to Cuba. The executive team thanked us for our time and said we'd hear back within a day from the regional director's office.

God did it again. He led me down a dead end. We went back to our hotel room, hoping to celebrate, but instead, I was just sad. Another delay. Another disappointment. Thanks to God. Maybe I had it all wrong. Maybe, I thought, my childhood experience was nothing more than pure emotionalism spurred on by youthful ignorance. What was I going to tell everyone? All of my new missionary friends? Was I going to say to them God screwed up? Or was I going to say I just got it all wrong? I didn't know what to do. All I knew was that I needed to be on assignment. We had to do something, anything. We had to be on the move.

I asked myself so many times why one would continue to pursue missions if there were so many obstacles? For starters, my life was already good. Why shake the floor (or as the Spanish saying says, *mover el piso*) and introduce so much difficulty? It honestly takes a special kind of person to see the glass half-full all the time. I once spoke to a counselor who said, "You know what, Bob? I think you're positive to a fault." She might have been right; however, without that level of positivity, I'd have given up a long time before on many, many blessings that seemed impossible if it weren't for God. But for missionary longevity, there must be a genuine call from God. Even though I couldn't hear, see, or feel God, I knew my call was real no matter what anyone said. Thank heavens I dared to trust in this God I was learning to follow, despite not understanding the God-process.

The next day, we received our invitation from the regional director to meet in his office. It was game-on. Upon arriving, I met my soon-to-be boss, Dick Nicholson. We went through the formalities of a first-time interview, after which he offered us a position in the country of Chile. When I initially applied, I applied as an evangelist, even though we learned an evangelist appointment may not pan out during our time in Missouri. That day in Dick's office, I found out that this was true. The Assemblies of God wouldn't send me as an evangelist. I was offered a position in Chile working to build God's church as a church planter.

I should have been ecstatic, but I didn't accept right away. There was no pressure to accept the offer, but I was told I could have a day to pray about it and give my answer. And that's what we did. With a twenty-four-hour deadline, there was no time to waste. I was clueless as to what to say. I knew absolutely nothing about the country. So, I went to Google. I started reading everything I could to become educated quickly about a country that was on my radar for the first time. As a couple, Michele and I talked about Chile together. Being in a two-week conference with many other missionary candidates gave us other friends to talk about it. We, of course, also took some time to talk to God about the proposition individually. And the time flew by fast. By the time the deadline approached, we were no closer to a decision. I had hoped for some moment of enlightenment, but it never came.

We walked into Dick's office the next day, still hoping that God would somehow illuminate our paths. Again, God was silent on the situation. Could it be that He wanted to know if I'd place my faith in that Holy Spirit calling moment I'd experienced as a young, naïve kid? Could it be that God needed to test my faith through this rejection and all those previous rejections before I ever stepped foot onto the mission field? If so, He was doing a pretty good job.

Faith is an essential aspect of following God. Hebrews devoted an entire chapter to applauding the faith of some of the greatest heroes of the Bible. Hebrews 11:7 tells how Noah built an ark to protect his family from a rainstorm that no one had experienced until then. The people thought he was crazy. Assuming scholars are right that no one had previously experienced rain, this man's building of a massive ship to endure an unknown event would have seemed like pure absurdity. We never read of God encouraging Noah verbally once he received his initial mission to build the ark. You never see God step on the scene and say, "Noah, I see their laughing, I see their mockery. Just keep doing what I told you in the beginning." No. God gives Noah the assignment, and

Noah had to endure God's silence during his assignment until the rain shows up many years later. I find that amusing.

God tells Abraham to sacrifice his son and then steps away to watch from a distance. Did God encourage Abraham as he climbed up the side of a mountain, fully prepared to murder his son in response to God's word? No. Abraham must have been fighting with God in his head, thinking, *God, I don't get you. Why won't you tell me something before it's too late?* God commanded Abraham to sacrifice Isaac and then disappeared from the scene until Abraham was about to strike his son.

Then, there's Moses. He saw God in a bush. Moses received his call from a bush that was on fire. Even though he was ill-prepared to handle the task, God said that "I am" would accompany him. Moses complained, saying to the bush, a fiery bush, the most spectacular God-miracle, "Who am I that I should go to Pharaoh and bring the Israelites out of Egypt?" (Exodus 3:11). Think of all the times Moses shook in his boots before the people wondering, *Where is God?*

Finally, think about the Israelites walking around Jericho. Hebrews 11:30 says they marched around the city's walls for seven days. What a bunch of looney God-followers. Think about what things looked like on day four, five, six, or even seven as they walked around a wall, seemingly alone. God told them what to do, and they simply did it. If I were them, I'd have thought, *We look ridiculous, and where is God? Will He do what He said?* People on the wall were probably laughing, jeering, and maybe even throwing things at them, and all the Israelites could say was, "God told us...."

The Bible is peppered with examples of people's faith and actions. God never told us we'd be exempt from seemingly absurd requests. He gave us these illustrations to guide us in our faith journey. We were never asked to be guided by blind faith. The myriad of examples in the Bible is meant to bolster our faith. People like you and me who listened to God while responding and acting in faith even when they wouldn't ever experience the promise itself. The writer of Hebrews says, "All these people were still living by faith when they died. They did not receive the things promised; they only saw them and welcomed them from a distance, admitting that they were foreigners and strangers on earth" (Hebrews 11:13). Part of being Spirit-led is understanding that God also has us on a journey much like these heroes of the faith in the Bible. That journey may involve us having a single encounter or ongoing encounters with Jesus; it may also have us respond to God by activating our faith.

As Michele and I sat there wrestling with God's lack of audible response, Dick asked, "Well, have you decided?"

I responded, "Dick, all I know is that God called us to be missionaries. If Chile is the door that God is opening, then that's the door we want to walk through."

I realized that we were in Missouri in response to that call for Cuba, even though it seemed like Cuba wouldn't be happening. I realized that Dick, the committee, and those with the Assemblies of God World Missions had heard our hearts and listened to our call. They, too, were seeking God along with us. Our application process wasn't a decision being taken lightly by anyone. I had to realize that God was speaking, although I possibly hadn't heard Him.

> Discernment in its fullness takes a practiced heart, fine-tuned to hear the Word of God and the single-mindedness to follow that Word in love. It is truly a gift from God, but not one dropped from the skies fully formed. It is a gift cultivated by a prayerful life and the search for self-knowledge.[16]

I believe any individual can miss God's directives, but in this case, a group of individuals was praying for our success. It was no longer just Bob and Michele. We had a whole host of people both praying and fasting for us. I had to realize that each one of the mission committee members had experience. They had a trajectory in missions. Each one of these people knew things that would take me years to learn. Maybe God was using them to help guide me in the right direction for ministry. Dick was the regional director for Latin America for a reason. I prayed He wasn't making hasty decisions. What did He know that I didn't know? I had to recognize that God never gave me the whole map of my mission journey. Looking back, I thank God for not giving me that map. I don't think He ever will—but He gave me the ability to act in faith. And active faith releases God's miracle-working power. That day, I realized God did speak. He spoke through the wisdom of the committee when they asked me, "Will you go to Chile?" The answer was an emphatic "Yes."

We said yes to the Assemblies of God World Missions, and we said yes to God. We said yes to missions. Would we ever go to Cuba? I really didn't know, but I settled for taking active steps and responded to a God-voice that came through the counsel of the World Missions Committee. Yes, throughout my application process, I experienced many unexpected delays and rejections, but here I was, finally getting my "Yes" opportunity. Someone once said, "The church in general panics when miracles miscarry." My interpretation of that statement is that people too sometimes panic when God's miracles miscarry. God's call to missions seemed clear when I was a kid. I had imagined a direct route from A to Z. I considered my experience with God a miracle. Just the fact that the God of the universe considered me for His service, that He would allow His Holy Spirit to dwell in me and allow me to experience His precious call when I was a child, was a miracle. But my interpretation of not being sent to Cuba was that God's miracle miscarried. I panicked—many times. I panicked through all of my rejections, and then there was the change to Chile. To me, it didn't seem like God knew what He was doing. Thankfully, God never got upset with me; He never got nervous. He knew these refining moments were of utmost importance. He knew that we all need an active faith. So that day, we said yes to Chile.

FUNDRAISING

*Depend on it. God's work done in God's way will never
lack God's supply. He is too wise a God to frustrate
His purposes for lack of funds, and He can just as
easily supply them ahead of time as afterwards,
and He much prefers doing so. — Hudson Taylor*

For the next fifteen months, I traveled all over the Northeastern United States. As a family, we almost lived in our little red van. After returning from Missouri as newly approved missionary candidates to Chile, things got real pretty fast. Candidates must raise the required finances to get to the mission field, and there's never a guarantee. Sadly, some don't make it. They either struggle to raise the money or decide this life is not for them.

Whatever the case, I knew it wasn't going to be easy. Look at everything I went through to convince Assemblies of God World Missions of my call. Now I had to call pastors who had no idea who I was. My church network was practically non-existent. The only network I had was the support of Assemblies of God World Missions in Missouri, the New Jersey Assemblies of God, and my pastor. I had to pray that God would help me with the rest. I'd have to talk to people from all walks of life to convince them that God had called us. I'd have to persuade churches to sponsor us financially so that we could make an important difference in Chile. While there's always the hope that God will send the right people or church to help you enter the mission field, it doesn't change the fact that God uses you as a person to communicate the vision.

When I was finally approved as a missionary, we had no funding, which meant I had to work until we could sustain ourselves. I was no fundraiser—I was a computer engineer. Fundraising was brand-new territory for me, and I was totally unprepared. Remember when Moses was standing at the burning bush? That was precisely how he felt that day. Unqualified. Unexperienced. Unable.

Are you ready to hear something that should blow your socks off? If you're willing to serve God, be prepared to understand that your call will depend on Him many times. When He gives you a vision or a purpose for life, that vision will often never reach maturity unless He does the impossible. If it's to be God-birthed and achieved, it needs to be God-empowered. That's what makes Him God. Moses was qualified, experienced and able, but he still needed God. Moses had to know and tell them, "I am has sent me" (Exodus 3:14). "I am" makes the difference. I had to believe that, too. We all have to believe that. For me to develop from being a missionary candidate to a fully-appointed missionary, God had to help me. He had to intervene.

Because I wasn't funded at that stage, I continued working my secular job to pay the bills. I also ministered incognito as a missionary on weekends and weeknights, speaking in church services. During my lunch hour, I went out to my car and worked through a massive church list, contacting Assembly of God churches, hoping they'd allow me to speak. I called everyone I possibly could. I left tons of messages, which meant many call-backs. I needed to keep everything under wraps because I needed my job. Urgent bathroom runs or secret closet conversations became the norm for answering calls.

Thank God, the telephone calling on my lunch hour paid off. I was booking lots of services, and before long, I had filled up our speaking schedule every Sunday morning, Sunday night, and Wednesday night. During the week, I traveled alone, but we loaded up the kids and traveled as a family on the weekends.

I celebrate my kids in this moment. They never chose to be missionaries, but they still had to follow their mom and dad, listening to sermon after sermon about missions. They lived in restaurants as their mom and dad shared their call for Chile with pastors. These were long, long days.

Most people don't know that we had no money for hotels, which meant the car became our daughters' hotel. During our travels, especially on Sunday afternoons, we'd find shady spots between services so that our daughters could nap in the car. This was our situation weekend after weekend for nearly fifteen months. It seemed like it was never-ending.

When the day finally came to resign from my secular job, I thought it would be the most challenging day ever. I was about to lose my salary I had worked so hard to attain. I was resigning my office and my tenure. I had a fantastic position that would soon belong to someone else. For those techies familiar with the software world, I was a Microsoft MCP, MCSE, Network +, A +, Novell CNA, and Cisco CCNA, CCNP, CCDA, and CCDP. These were sought-after and hard-earned certifications. I had hoped to achieve the coveted Cisco CCIE before my resignation, but after failing it twice, I gave up my final conquest. There were about ten thousand CCIEs worldwide at the time, and I really wanted to join the club as I made my exit from computers. That would have been my crowning achievement, but it will be a victory for another day.

I wondered how I was going to resign. I went to my employer's office and asked for a moment. Joe Montero, my boss, was a believer; but still, I wasn't sure how he was going to respond. I said, "Joe, I've been keeping a secret from you. I'm now an approved missionary with the Assemblies of God. For the past few months, I've been fundraising during my off-hours. I have been scheduling speaking meetings with various churches. Joe, our family is planning on serving as foreign missionaries in Santiago." Just then, the weight lifted. I did it! I was surprised at how easy it was, how awesome it felt. There was no going back.

How did Joe respond? He asked me this question I'll never forget, "Bob, is it your salary? If so, how much do you want to earn? Whatever it is, we'll make it happen."

Great, I thought. *I'm making the hardest decision of my life, and you're offering me more money.* But I said, "Joe, it's not about the money. I'm taking a huge salary cut, and life is about to change drastically for us."

By the end of the conversation, Joe asked me for a sponsorship form, and to this day, he has been one of our faithful supporters. God will put great people in your life as you grow. I encourage you to learn everything you can from them. Joe is one of those people. He led our department amazingly well, and I learned some great leadership lessons from him. Joe, thank you!

My resignation letter was accepted that same day. Because of my seniority, the company didn't terminate my employment that day. I stayed on for a few more weeks, training my successors. People at the company were dumbfounded. How? Why? What? "Bob, you're an idiot," some people muttered.

I must confess, I didn't understand where our faith was taking us. I now realize that I was in the dark about so many things. Michele and I knew we had to move and do something because God had called us, both of us. I see the past much clearer now. So much more makes sense, but I needed the darkness, the rejections, the trials, and everything else that came with following Jesus. Jesus reminded us in John 16:33, "In this world you will have trouble. But take heart! I have overcome the world." Jesus wanted us to know that following Him never meant avoiding the difficulty of facing our humanity.

Jesus knows we all need to face unavoidable challenges. Sometimes, we create those challenges because of our decisions. Sometimes these challenges come from circumstances beyond our control, and sometimes God sends these challenges to refine and grow us. If you're following Jesus and find that there are no challenges or roadblocks in the way, you might want to check if you're following the Jesus of the Bible. Everyone has to grow. And you won't grow without the right circumstances. Sadly, hardships often accompany those circumstances that encourage us to grow, and we must overcome these challenges. God is a good God. That's why He requires growth from every one of us. Paul, the apostle, once chastised the Corinthians (3:1-3) about him having to give them milk instead of solid food. He tells them, "...you are still worldly" (v.3). Essentially, Paul said God's design is for you to mature.

As we carried out our ongoing fundraising, I soon realized that my first rejections were helpful. They taught me to struggle with God and myself to discern whether my call was, in fact, a call from God. We typically don't consider difficulties to be helpful, and I'm not talking about difficulties created because of our actions.

The following example can give us a clearer picture. Recently, I was with a pastor friend who had established a great Bible-believing church a few years ago. This brother loved the Lord, and I'd say one hundred percent committed to his faith. I was often in awe of his faith. Even as a struggling church, the congregation was committed to missions, especially to our family. However, a few years into the church, it became clear that the church was not taking off as he expected. They were preaching the Word of God. They were praying. They seemed to be doing, from a spiritual viewpoint, everything right; yet, they struggled for survival. As we talked over a meal, I began to understand why they struggled the way they did. This brother was very set in his ways of doing church. In fact, many aspects of his church life came from the church experience he had growing up in another cultural context. His idea of worship didn't allow for any expressions other than the ones he experienced in his formative years. His preaching style had not evolved in a way that connected with the surrounding community.

Let's be clear; I'm not advocating a "compromised" church. But the church must understand its community. Without compromising the gospel's integrity, the church must adapt to its cultural context and communicate in a relevant and uncompromising way with its members.

Based on the facts of what I saw and experienced, the struggles this church faced were self-imposed. Yet, when this brother heard me preaching about struggles, he was encouraged to keep fighting his battles. The problem was the battles he was fighting weren't necessarily meant to be fought. He had discerned from a message I preached that he should stay fighting and keep doing what he had been doing all along. I wanted to scream out, "No!" I believed God had been taking me through storms of rejection to help make sure I was committed to my call. But in this pastor's case his storms were entirely self-imposed. Unfortunately, he failed to understand that his actions were putting roadblocks in the church's path. He felt that the difficulties were just a part of the process, and he was determined to push on in the same direction after hearing my message.

Hearing God takes work. Self-imposed obstacles are frustrating, but God-imposed obstacles can create the most incredible beauty out of ashes. You must work to hear God. You have to work at having conversations with God, pausing long enough to listen to His message. Sometimes a challenge means abandoning ship; other times, it means changing course, but there are also times when it means you have to stay the course because God is in control.

Discernment is crucial and not easily learned; it takes practice, practice, and more practice. Hearing God takes work. I'm no expert in hearing from God, but I'm thankful I managed to learn how to abandon ship, correct course, or continue straight ahead when it counted. These three ideas are exactly what I learned from the very beginning of fundraising. There were many days, more than I'd like to count, when I felt like I should abandon ship. I can't tell you how many times I thought, *Bob, there's no way you'll raise the money you need, You don't know enough people,* or *You are out of your league with this.* These thoughts bothered me for days.

There were days I needed to correct my course. I met a man sent by the New Jersey Assemblies of God, and he helped me overcome my fundraising challenges. When I felt like I was failing, I sought help. Remember, you'll never win the God-race alone. You need people. The right people. This man helped me to course-correct.

But then there were days I just knew to keep pushing on.

You're in a storm, but it's a God-storm, and He gives you the green light to stay the course. Just push on straight ahead. It will happen. I am grateful for one mentor in my life. He has spoken many words of encouragement and has even spoken into my kids' lives. This man is still my mentor and a fantastic blessing to my life, even though we've never met in person. His name is Zig Ziglar. We met through a CD at "Automobile University." He was just one of the many voices in my life, but he was a gem. In isolation, you'll die. You never know; just one conversation may attune your ears so that you hear God for the first time. Hearing God takes work.

That first fundraising cycle as new missionary candidates led us through some deep waters of faith, but it also allowed us to see God work in some most marvelous ways.

After I resigned from my secular job, our fundraising efforts slowed. Soon after that, we used up the money we had amassed in our account. For the first time, we were dealing with a negative bank balance; however, this time, I had no outside job to pay our bills.

We were new missionaries, and this would be the first of several times that we would walk through a challenging financial situation in the ministry. We were a young couple with two kids, so I sent out a newsletter to our few supporters and asked for two things. First, I asked for them to pray for us to connect with new friends with a heart for missions. Second, I asked them if they'd be willing to send a one-time, special offering to help us overcome our financial hurdle. To my surprise, two of my family members in Deerfield, New Jersey, responded to our email request. These two special people were Uncle Rudy and Aunt Helene.

My aunt and uncle were huge missions supporters. When they arrived in the United States many years earlier, they were very closely involved in establishing the German Assemblies of God in southern New Jersey. They lived and breathed missions. It was just part of their DNA as a mom, dad, husband, wife, and as church members. My aunt Helene responded, "Bob, Uncle Rudy and I want to send you guys a gift of $1,000." My aunt and uncle supported us for nearly twenty years before they went home to be with the Lord. God may not have spoken to my aunt Helene that day, but when she called me, it was as if God were reminding me that you can't do missions alone.

In fact, you can't do life alone. You'll experience discouragements and rejections; life will happen. So, what do you do when you're all alone? You sink, you get discouraged, and you may even abandon your faith. God created the church for a reason. It's a place of discipleship where we learn about Him, but it's also much more than that. God wants us to know Him and not just learn about Him. In church, we learn to know God by wrestling with His teachings in community.

As a matter of fact, we grow into maturity through at least two avenues. We take the first avenue when we each use our gifts in the context of the church. When we use our gifts, we understand better how our gifts work with us. The second avenue involves learning to live in community, which is possibly one of the most challenging components of church life. Whenever there are different groups of people, conflict is bound to occur. It's inevitable.

For starters, look at marriage. You can't get married and expect never to have conflict. If there's never conflict in the marriage, at least one person is living a lie. I think one of the most important aspects of marriage is that you have the opportunity to learn to be a follower of Jesus Christ.

At times you have to ask forgiveness; at other times, you need to submit. There might even be times where you have to tame that tongue that gets you into trouble. You can't have a happy, fulfilled marriage if you don't learn how to give and take. And in that process, there's often some level of conflict.

The same applies to the church. When working in a community, you have to learn the gentle war of giving and taking. It teaches you to become a better follower of Jesus—gentle, meek, longsuffering, patient, kind. Can you go to heaven without ever going to church? Yes, your salvation doesn't depend on going to church, but you can't have a happy, fulfilled life until you truly learn to follow Jesus. Learning to follow Jesus can never occur in isolation. We need people to refine us, sharpen us, and mold us into the image of Christ. Even Paul said, "Imitate me as I imitate Christ." There's something valuable to be said about living in community, going to church, and following Jesus Christ. You can't do missions alone, and you can't do life alone and expect to achieve all that God has in store for you.

Many financial miracles happened during that first fundraising cycle, but miracles didn't stop there. By May 2006, we had raised our budget. For a rookie fundraiser like me, this was a life-changing miracle! There were times when I thought the constant speaking and traveling would never end. So did my wife and kids. But we made it. We got through our fundraising cycle in fifteen months.

In 2 Kings 4, we read about a widowed woman who struggled with a financial need beyond her control. She cried out to the prophet Elisha for help because her dead husband's creditor was coming to take her boys as slaves. Rather than just perform a miracle, Elisha says, "How can I help you? Tell me, what do you have in your house?" (v.2). He probed for a solution that he could use to activate her faith. He didn't want her to idly expect God to do something with no action on her part. How often do we act the same way? We pray, but we don't act or move. Yet, when we read the Bible, we can't help but see that a faith action is what moved God to intervene in the lives of His people in many instances. This woman says, "Elisha, all I have is a small olive oil jug" (v. 2). Here's the key: Elisha capitalized on what she had and what she could do.

Elisha was moved by the woman's request and says, "Okay, take that jug, round up other jugs from your neighbors, go in your house, shut the door, and start pouring" (2 Kings 4:3-7). When she acted, the miracle was made real. Not before—rather, right at the moment she asked, believed, and obeyed. As soon as she obeyed, the oil ran until she could fill every jug in her house. I wish I had been there to see that. But God put it in His Word so we could read it, be encouraged, and learn that active faith is crucial for hearing and experiencing God. After the jugs were filled, Elisha gave her an action step. Sell. Then and only then would she have the money she needed.

Miracles serve a purpose. God will never perform miracles just for the sake of performing them. In my case, I needed those miracles that were linked to my faith actions to help remind me that God was in control. While I never experienced the miracle of the non-emptying oil jug, I experienced the ongoing provision of a God who is faithful in fulfilling His Word.

The Law of Economics

If you're in a financial bind, you need to recognize that God can move mountains. God can provide in ways beyond human understanding; that's simply His way. Here's the problem: many folks confess, "My God shall supply all my needs" (Philippians 4:19). They pray for provision, and they may even recite the Scripture out of Malachi 3:10, which says, "the Lord would throw open the floodgates of heaven to pour out a blessing." These individuals sadly use the words of Scripture out of context. They give meaning to verses that God never intended.

I once counseled a pastor who told me about a verse in the Bible where Timothy started one of his letters, "I pray that you would prosper and be in good health..." From that one verse, the pastor formed a prosperity mindset that colored his thinking about money. He told me, "Roberto, that means God will bless us financially, and we don't need to experience lack. It says it right there, 'I pray that you would prosper and be in good health.'" He was adamant that God promised every follower of Jesus financial prosperity with that one verse. That's a teaching for another day, but it does make it clear that we first need to have a good understanding of the whole of the Scriptures.

We can make isolated Bible verses say just about anything we want. But, again, when we wrestle with our faith in community, we can learn to dig into God's Word with other people that can help us understand the whole of the Scriptures. Then, when we understand the whole of the Scriptures, we begin to understand the role of our decision-making processes along with God's provision-making power.

There may be instances where living expenses may be beyond our control, and we need a God intervention. However, some people fail to budget according to their needs spending frivolously on their wants rather than needs (for instance, buying a $60,000 truck when they can only afford a $3,500 used Honda Civic). Maybe they're so concerned with living their best life that they sacrifice their long-term well-being for short-term material gains (such as buying a $200,000 house when they can only afford a $75,000 house). They let their eyes make all of the financial decisions. If I live beyond my means because of poor decision-making, how can I expect God to take up my slack?

To illustrate, at the beginning of my marriage, I felt we needed to have new furniture and a nice home stereo unit even though we couldn't afford it. The easiest solution to that problem was to buy on credit. As a result, this one mistake kept us in bondage for many years. Credit-card offers came daily when I first graduated high school. The financial world loves to keep us captive, but no one will make you become a slave. TV, the culture in general, and the internet can all tempt us to become a slave to money. Still, the only one who makes that decision is us. I almost didn't become a missionary because of bad money habits. Thankfully, I can honestly say God helped us. But only after I got my act together; it was a grueling process.

I began to follow the earthly laws of economics, and it paid off. I gave God something with which He could work, and He helped me. I started following Dave Ramsey's *Financial Peace University* (which I fully recommend). I discovered his program through my local church! Amen to the local church. Michele and I began living on the envelope system advocated in the book. To this day, we still live on the envelope system with a calculated monthly budget to the last penny. To God be the glory, that debt-free lifestyle wasn't only for us and our benefit. That debt-free lifestyle allowed us to be generous, tithe, support missions, and feel at ease when God prompted us to give to a cause.

Keep Moving Forward

Eventually, May 6, 2006, arrived—the day we were finally given clearance to leave for the mission field. That date came because of the goodness of God. He gave us one hundred percent success during our fundraising cycle, which meant that it was finally time to leave the United States. We'd take our first steps onto the mission field, not as missionary candidates but rather as fully-appointed, fully-funded missionaries. Again, it was because of God, because of people, and because we daily put our faith into action. At this point, the next, most amazing miracle happened.

But first, I need to unpack the context surrounding that miracle. Earlier that year, Michele and I met with a longtime friend, Joe Vélez. He was establishing a brand-new Spanish church within an American church. Meetings were held in a borrowed facility with primarily first-generation Hispanic immigrants. Most people were from Mexico, but many countries were represented. My role in the church was as the minister of music. God didn't tell me to participate in this new work, and my wife wasn't a big supporter either. Finally, she told me very hesitantly, "Bob, we just recently got out of a bad situation at the Camden church. Things are going well with our new church, and we're involved. Why do we need to do something more?" For me, it wasn't about doing something more; it was about doing something I believed would help us in pursuing our missions call. First-generation Spanish immigrants, no English, a new church plant—it seemed like an exciting opportunity for which we were well suited.

Boy, did I pray. "God, what do you want me to do? If you don't want me to help out, please say no, shut the door, close down the opportunity, and make it impossible." But God did none of those things. Sometimes it seems opportunities present themselves, and you just know they are right for you. Other times, we shouldn't rush our decision-making. Even if it seems right, we still need to pray, seek God, and be sensitive for that moment when God speaks.

What happens when He doesn't? Could it be He uses a God-silence as a tool to see if we'll keep walking forward? When Jesus was in the Garden of Gethsemane, He was sweating drops of blood. He knew His crucifixion lay ahead, and He asked God, "Father, if you are willing, take this cup from me; yet not my will, but yours be done" (Luke 22:42). He knew He had to walk down this road, yet He still asked God to change His circumstances. We never hear God respond, "Son, this is the only way; you have to endure the pain and walk the way of the cross." In fact, we see no reply.

And yet Jesus says, "Not my will, but yours be done." He was willing to obey even when there were moments of silence. One of my greatest life lessons is the understanding that there will be times when God is silent, but still speaking. That may seem very contradictory, yet it makes a ton of sense. His silence may be so clear, yet He puts a burning desire in us to act according to His will. In essence, He speaks without speaking. If you don't allow yourself to become sensitized to God's spoken and unspoken voice, you'll miss the cues. For me, I felt the desire to help this church was a God-cue. Ultimately, Michele came around. I talked to my pastor, and we started helping out with the services on Friday nights, broken Spanish and all.

I didn't play any instruments. I took saxophone lessons as a boy, but nothing at all related to church music. So, being the new minister of music, I arranged music sets, practiced with the singers, and developed a team of individuals that didn't exist when we started. I didn't have any musicians at the time and had to make do with track background music; however, I didn't like that solution for a live church service. It works well for some churches, but it didn't work for me. I just didn't like it.

Again, it was time to take another step of faith. Four weeks later, I bought a guitar and a chord book. Believe it or not, within a few short weeks, I was playing a pitiful guitar rendition of church music. I was leading the music ministry with such a broken Spanish that I don't know how anyone understood me.

God has a sense of humor. Here's what happened. People began to tell me that they played guitar or piano or any other musical instrument. I thought, "Awesome, let's get you playing." And that's how we started. God used my extravagant faith to pull people out of the pews and into their giftings.

Now here's the best part. We began to form great friendships with people our age. One of those friends was Jimmy. Jimmy came from Costa Rica all alone to achieve the American dream. He lived in Philadelphia but traveled to New Jersey to be a part of this great body of believers. He worked in a job unrelated to the church, but he had a passion for God. Over time, our friendship developed into something special, and it became clear that God was ready to show me exactly how He prepared our steps. This all happened even while we were oblivious to what He was doing. The next, most amazing miracle was now ready to unfold.

LANGUAGE SCHOOL

The depth of desire has a great deal to do with the outcome of our life. Often, those who accomplish what they set out to do in life are not those who are the most talented or gifted or who have had the best opportunities. Often they are the ones who are most deeply in touch with how badly they want whatever they want; they are the ones who consistently refuse to be deterred by the things that many of us allow to become excuses.[17]

The Assemblies of God training base for language and culture is located in San Jose. Here, every new missionary spends nearly one year acquiring the necessary tools for success in their missions call to Latin America and the Caribbean.

We arrived in Costa Rica to spend the next twelve months learning Spanish and Latin American culture before going on to Chile in South America.

We lived right on the grounds of the language school with a group of other missionaries. It was like experiencing high school for the second time. God, please never send me to high school again! The Spanish acquisition came easy. Michele and I had a good understanding of the language; however, husbands and wives should never be in the same Spanish class, especially when they come from New Jersey. We quickly had to learn that if we were going to survive the year, we had to stop correcting each other. I can't say, even all these years later, that we ever mastered that lesson.

The challenge for our kids was a little different. Our little Isabella was only around two years old when she came to Costa

Rica. She attended daycare while we were in school. It was more than simply daycare; it was designed for her to learn Spanish as well. From the first day, the teachers greeted her in Spanish. That first day was a full immersion in Spanish. The teachers spoke no English. So, she was forced to communicate in Spanish even when she didn't know how to use the language. It's no wonder Isabella fought us so much about speaking Spanish as she grew up. As soon as she knew someone spoke English, she'd never let you hear her speak Spanish.

Priscilla, on the other hand, went to an English-run school where most of the students were Costa Rican. Her dilemma was that she needed to learn in English, but if she wanted to be friends with the other students, she had to learn Spanish to fit in. So, she learned Spanish. Today, both of my kids are fluent in Spanish. It may not have been their choice, but God uses that gift in their lives to this day.

Academically, things went well for us. Spanish acquisition was fairly easy. Still, I wanted a broader vocabulary and wanted to speak Spanish well. So even though the Spanish came easy, it didn't exempt me from studying to be the best Spanish speaker I could be. I did whatever I could to learn, to grow. My focus was on becoming the best version of myself within my new host culture.

When we first arrived in Costa Rica, I remembered Jimmy had said, "Bobby, when you get to my country, you have to meet my family. They want to meet you." So, I thought, *Sure thing*. But I didn't understand, at that time, the gravity of that meeting.

When I finally did pick up the phone to call Jimmy's brother Jamms, we set a date for their family and ours to connect. It was unbelievable that in an entire country the size of West Virginia, Jimmy's family lived about a mile from where we stayed.

Initially, our connection with Jimmy's family seemed like a coincidence. His family and ours, their proximity to the language school, the church in the United States, all just pure coincidence. But truthfully, God was setting the stage to provide for us an incredibly miraculous missions career.

We took a taxi ride to Jimmy's family's house one weekend, and that's when God started an amazing friendship that remains strong to this day. These new friends, the Espinoza-Marín family, would become our family. His dad Esdras and mom Hilda received us as if we were their own kids. In Costa Rica, you don't just make friends or go to someone's house on a whim. To be invited to someone's house for an intimate meal is an honor. In this culture, it's a symbol of moving beyond acquaintances to becoming close friends. That first night at their house, I made some major Spanish mistakes that bring a smile to my face as I think about our friendship. Apparently, I accused the taxi driver of vulgar behavior, and I somehow said I smoked weed. They must have thought, *Bless his heart, at least he is trying.*

Our visits became a weekend tradition. They fed us and spent a lot of time with us. They became our family. Their church became our church, and here's the most amazing part. Remember how people weren't casually invited to other people's houses, especially if they didn't know each other? Because the Espinoza-Marín family were our friends, all of their friends immediately became our friends. This opportunity gave us an incredible circle of local Costa Rican friends, which meant we didn't have to try so hard to make friends at the language school, but for me, that was okay. I was there to learn Spanish, to learn the culture, to become a missionary.

Always Treasure Focus

Remember how Nehemiah faced a wall that was in crumbles? He knew he had a mission to complete. However, he also knew that to succeed in his mission, he had to make sure that he didn't focus primarily on his obstacles. In Nehemiah chapter 4, we read:

> Sanballat was very angry when he learned that we were rebuilding the wall. He flew into a rage and mocked the Jews,[2] saying in front of his friends and the Samarian army officers, "What does this bunch of

poor, feeble Jews think they're doing? Do they think they can build the wall in a single day by just offering a few sacrifices? Do they actually think they can make something of stones from a rubbish heap—and charred ones at that?" Tobiah the Ammonite, who was standing beside him, remarked, "That stone wall would collapse if even a fox walked along the top of it!"

The obstacles were real. Failure was just as real. However, Nehemiah realized he had a mission, an assignment to complete. Instead of being discouraged or downtrodden, he prayed (verse 4), and then he pushed on. Verse 6 says, "At last the wall was completed to half its height around the entire city." Despite that forward motion, Nehemiah was still met with the following:

But when Sanballat and Tobiah and the Arabs, Ammonites, and Ashdodites heard that the work was going ahead and that the gaps in the wall of Jerusalem were being repaired, they were furious. They all made plans to come and fight against Jerusalem and throw us into confusion (v. 7–8).

What I love about Nehemiah is that he teaches us the importance of focus when being on assignment. He worked hard to avoid becoming a victim of life's distractions. He knew the only way to complete his assignment was to focus on following God. Our language school was a lesson in focus.

Time spent with my new family was out of this world. We went on trips together and experienced life as Costa Ricans. Obviously, I'd never be able to experience some things as a foreigner, but I did my best to immerse myself fully in the culture. I praise our awesome God for sending the Espinoza-Marín family our way. Their children became our friends; it was just a miracle made in heaven. Jamms, Jhonn, Dyhana, and Jeffry were more than just Jimmy's siblings; they were our new family.

For the next twelve months, language school served to be an invaluable tool. It gave us the ability, as long as we took advantage of it, to connect with our new family in ways that few ever do. We learned the Spanish language and culture by day, and by night, God gave us a gift that was so precious I'll never be able to repay Him.

Finally, the day had to come when the language school journey would be over. Just like Nehemiah stayed on assignment and finished his wall, we finished language school. It was time to move on because Chile waited for us. With only three days before we left Costa Rica, I had to move out of the language school. I knew I had to keep my expenses to a minimum, so I found a hotel for forty dollars per night. Just before leaving language school, I went to talk to the language school's director.

"Jay, it's been great. Since we're leaving, I found a place to stay downtown called Hotel Rey." I was proud of myself. It was cheap, close to everything, and most importantly, close to our new family.

Jay's eyes grew large. "Bob, I don't think you want to stay there."

"Why?" I asked.

He grimaced as he spoke, "Hotel Rey is not just a hotel."

His raised eyebrows and look of concern caused me to ask why.

"It's...well..., it's like a nightclub..." He cleared his throat and lowered his voice. "It's actually a brothel." He sat and waited for my reaction.

I was speechless. To think I was going to take my daughters there. Sometimes you don't know what you don't know. I found out prostitution was very real in Costa Rica. I also learned that downtown San Jose is divided into areas assigned to different kinds of prostitution and clientele. You'll find ladies, crossdressers, pimps, locals, and even foreigners there. Depending on the downtown area, you will find a different clientele with a corresponding difference in price points. I didn't know any of this even though I had lived there for the past twelve months.

I was sheltered in many ways but not blind. Even though I was unaware of how prostitution and trafficking worked in

Costa Rica, I often saw signs of it. Today, the laws have become much more stringent. That's a good thing. Costa Rica has made some incredible leaps forward in legislation focused on curbing human trafficking.

I can still remember awkward moments that raised our antennae when Michele and I, along with our daughters, would be sitting in restaurants and see older, gray-haired Americans sitting with very young girls. Many times, it appeared as though neither could communicate in the other's language. They just sat and ate.

There used to be a place called the "Good News Cafe," which had the best breakfasts. It seemed to draw Americans because I only ever saw American men sitting with beautiful, provocatively dressed women. While I didn't know the extent to which prostitution or trafficking existed, there was an inner warning that something was wrong. These women dressed in a way that was sure to draw attention, which didn't feel right.

I didn't know that my wife was feeling God tug on her heart for this area of ministry. We didn't really talk about it, but when seeing these odd couples of Americans and Costa Ricans, both young and old, it was easy to sense that something was wrong. These were conversations we never had. We didn't talk about this tug on her heart, and it was only later that I discovered how God brought fruition to a feeling he gently, but quietly impressed upon Michele.

Now aware that the Hotel Rey wasn't going to work, we had to develop a plan B. In talking with our Costa Rican family, they said, "Why don't you stay with us?" They didn't have a big house, and they were by no means wealthy, but they were always there for us in whatever we needed.

God met our needs again, and that's what we did. Michele bunked with Dyhana and the kids. I don't really remember where I slept, but I remember hearing the wooden bed squeaking with every movement throughout the night. We had to yell back and forth across the rooms, making the best of the situation. We knew that in just a short while, we might never see the Espinoza-

Marín family again.

Missionaries are constantly moving, and many goodbyes are wearing, so it was bittersweet that final night in their house. We knew we were heading to the place God had prepared for us, but we also knew we were leaving behind one of the most precious gifts God had ever given us, the Espinoza-Marín family.

We woke up that final morning with both excitement and sadness in our hearts. I don't think we could have ever pictured Costa Rica playing out that way. It wasn't like Costa Rica was just a steppingstone on our journey. God had put special people in our lives because we collaborated with a Spanish church plant in the United States. He knew what He was doing when I asked about that plant with those infamous words, "If you don't want me to help out, please say no, shut the door, close down the opportunity, or make it impossible." Remember, God did none of those things. He stayed silent, but because I recognized the God-deposited passion for helping amid the silence, Costa Rica turned out to be one of the most incredible years in setting us up for a fantastic mission success story.

OUR FIRST ASSIGNMENT

As we traverse down the path of God's leading,
secondary words and confirmations about what we
are undertaking will come...As the Spirit speaks to
us and we follow His leading, we won't get the whole
picture immediately. Doing something...requires
a keen ear and deep obedience.[18]

Our flight to Santiago lasted around twelve hours with a layover in Peru. While in Peru during the quick layover, we had our first ever interaction ever with a Chilean national. During the two years after we left Dick Nicholson's office, we embarked on a fifteen-month fundraising journey, traveled to San Jose where, for the next twelve months, God equipped us for ministry, and at the same time, God gave us a new family who helped us understand Latin America. Still, it was during this pitstop in Peru with a Chilean national that we realized, "You're not in Kansas anymore, Toto." Once we landed, most passengers deplaned while others stayed aboard for the immediate connecting flight to Santiago.

Now, when you travel internationally, you have a lot of bags. Those lots of bags mean lots of money. We were new missionaries, but my kids were troopers. At three and six years old, they had become my little human mules. They had free backpacks and carry-ons. From my experience, we never weighed those bags. What did I do? During the packing, I picked out the heaviest items, and I loaded up the kids. To this day, they still joke about what I put them through as we trekked through Latin America. I can still clearly remember how Isabella fell backward because her bag was too heavy to carry. Priscilla tried to help, but I had her barely standing up straight from the weight. I told the kids, "Girls, whatever you do, don't let anyone touch your bags! Don't let any flight stewardess try to load them into the overhead compartments." I have to laugh. Thankfully, we had no problems other than two tired kids. They were awesome, truly awesome. God gave me great kids. Yes, they complained, but who can blame them. Think about it. A forty-pound kid with an eighty-pound book bag. What was I thinking? And then came Peru.

We stayed on the plane, but we were supposed to change seats. I didn't know (and I didn't want to change my seat because of our bags). Then the new crew came on board when it happened.

A passenger stopped at my row, looked at his ticket, and said, "I think you're in my seat."

"Sorry, sir," I replied, "I think you're mistaken."

At this point, we were all speaking in Spanish.

"Stewardess! Stewardess!" he yelled.

I thought, *Oh man, we're toast.*

The guy was straightforward and not very tactful. I felt like he heard my Spanish and thought, *You repugnant foreigner, who do you think you are? You're in my world now; you're heading to my country of Chile, now ubícate* (you'd better recognize). He showed us his ticket with his seat number. Needless to say, I lost the battle, and he got the seat. But that was okay; no one ever made me move my overhead luggage. Thank God.

We soon learned that Chileans weren't like Central Americans. I struggled to understand their Spanish. It's the most beautiful accent I ever heard. Having a secret crush on Chilean Spanish, I wish I could speak like them. Michele and I often conversed with people, then compared notes on what we understood from the conversations. It's pretty funny. Looking back, I'd argue that you could understand any Spanish speaker if you understand this Chilean Spanish.

Chileans are unique. They say that they don't even speak Spanish; they speak "Castellano." The Chilean culture flourishes at night, whereas in Costa Rica, it is up early, to bed early. Chilean events usually take place from 8 PM to 10 PM. And this was my first experience. It unnerved me, and I had many concerns and questions about the future. "God, did we make the right decision to come here?" Often in moments like these, the devil likes to throw doubt and remind us of our past failures or flaws. The devil was quick to remind me God never told me He had planned Chile for my life. All I knew was Cuba and missions. Cuba wasn't happening, but our mission to Chile was. So, after taking our new seats, we slept until we arrived in Santiago the next morning.

Our Arrival

We woke up to a glorious sunrise with our plane landing at the Arturo Merino Benítez International Airport. I was smiling from ear to ear. I couldn't believe we were finally in Chile. We had no idea where we were going to live, nor had we met any of the missionaries with whom we were going to work. Once again, we were flying blind.

Have you ever seen all of those people at the airport holding nametags or pictures? That was our next step. Thankfully I saw two people holding a sign with my name on it. They introduced themselves as Mike and Dodey Files and said they'd be our missionary mentors for the next two years. We hugged these strangers, and they immediately became our new family. They collected our bags and took us to our apartotel (Airbnb). They stocked our refrigerator so that we'd have some food until we could do our shopping. I think the best thing they bought was Watts jelly, which is my all-time favorite jelly to this day. They even gifted us with two Chile Starbucks mugs as a welcoming present.

We were at our temporary home in the heart of Santiago. Mike and Dodey had left so we could get some rest. But who rests when you get to a new country on your new assignment?

We explored the surrounding areas walking up and down the streets as a family, visiting Falabellas, Paris, Mamút, and the local grocery store. I figured Chile was a coastal country, so why not get some seafood? That night is one of the most memorable nights we'd ever experience in Chile. We went back home and cooked the most delicious, fresh clams we've ever eaten. We turned on the radio to discover our newest favorite station, Amadeus, a smooth jazz channel with great tunes. We made it a family night.

The apartment was like a galley way. The floors were made of some sort of linoleum, which made them very slippery. Michele and I took turns dancing with the kids, trying to make Chile a place they'd love. We set up pseudo-bowling pins at one end of the apartment, and I then wrapped our girls in blankets and "threw them" down the galley way in our homemade bowling alley.

The phone rang, and we wondered who was calling us. I could hardly understand the person, but I gathered from the call that the neighbors complained about the noise coming from the Pérez domain. I think it was the front desk asking us to keep it down. But we didn't. It was way too much fun that night. I still have the videos on our computer. The kids were happy, we were happy, and if even for a moment, all of our concerns took a back seat for the sake of our family and fun.

Chilean Assemblies of God General Council

Then Uncle Mike came. Most missionaries have their kids refer to the other missionaries as aunts and uncles. This doesn't always happen, but it's a tradition that has existed in the Assemblies of God for many years. That second day, Uncle Mike arrived and said, "Bob, right now the General Council of the Chilean Assemblies of God is meeting. We'd like for you and Michele to go meet the leadership."

We had arrived in the country a few days before. I reminded him we didn't know anyone to hire as a babysitter. Mike said, "I'll arrange for a babysitter. You have nothing to worry about."

Nothing to worry about? We were only a few days into a new country. How were we going to leave our daughters with pure strangers? I was uncomfortable in making the decision. At that time, we were the only missionaries with little kids in Chile. Many of our colleagues were older, and they had not had to face these issues for many years, but it was new and fresh for us. There was no way. If you recall from chapter 1, that was the moment my mom decided to visit us and surprise the kids as their nanny for the week. What I failed to tell you was that my mom worked as a nurse without a fixed schedule. She could design her schedule to fit with her lifestyle. It makes me smile to think how God guided my mom into a career path that allowed her the flexibility to make such last-minute decisions. Not only did God begin to prepare me for missions as a young boy, but He also prepared my mom strategically in her career.

The morning my mom showed up at the apartotel, we surprised the kids. They were waiting in the living room, expecting their first Chilean babysitter to come walking through the front door. They went wild when their grandmom walked through the front door.

Now we were ready to head to General Council. This was where, for the very first time, God would speak a word, helping us realize we were in the correct country at the right time. When I had my interview with Dick Nicholson in Missouri a few years earlier, I had learned that going to Cuba as an evangelist, or any other country for that matter, was impossible. I remember thinking, *But God, when you called me, I felt you impress on me the importance of Cuba and the ministry of an evangelist, yet neither is happening. I don't understand.* God didn't need for me to understand. The truth is, had I understood what was taking place that day, the moment that was about to happen in Chile probably wouldn't have been all that powerful. Walking into the meeting at General Council, I knew no one. I didn't know the missionaries, nor did I know anyone from the national church. They approved my arrival, yet they had no idea who I was.

Mike was honestly the only person who could help me that day. For the next two years, Mike opened many doors for me. He was a big reason for the success we achieved in Chile. However, while he was the only one who had any idea who this new guy Roberto was, he didn't know that Dick had told me that I could forget about becoming an evangelist. Mike let the church leadership know I was there attending the general council meeting. And then the time finally came that I was to be introduced to the country's national church. Talk about a big moment. Just about every Assemblies of God pastor was present, and I was ready to greet everyone.

Then it happened. The superintendent said, "We have a new missionary evangelist in our midst, Roberto Pérez."

I was ecstatic. I could hardly believe that a conversation between myself and God was somehow whispered to the superintendent and now broadcast to the entire country. My jaw dropped, and my heart leaped out of my chest. No one ever said anything about being an evangelist for the Chilean Assemblies of God! I was told it would never happen, yet when the time came for us to meet the church, God spoke loud and clear through the superintendent, "New missionary evangelists." I was in awe. God had been silent about confirming Chile for nearly two years, but the day I met the church, He let me know He was wholly involved in my assignment. When I thought, *Am I in the right place?* God confirmed loudly, "Yes, you are."

As I've said so many times, God always used people in the process. It started with God using my new superintendent, Pepe, as His mouthpiece, but many other people were also involved in my first term. God used many special people to bless my life and remind me of my calling. We went to Chile, not because God's directions were clear to us, but because He gave me a childhood experience, followed by faith action steps. The Holy Spirit is real. He blows where He wants, and He works as He desires, but He will never make a mistake. Trust God. Trust the process. Your assignment is waiting, and He will speak! You have to begin to move; you have to do something—and allow God to do the rest.

That day at our Assemblies of God General Council marked the start of a term that would knock my socks off from beginning to end. To this day, I owe a ton of gratitude to my Chilean friends. The national church was valuable in forming who we are as missionaries today. Even though I learned early on that Chile was unlike the Caribbean nations of Latin America, the Chilean culture was instrumental in forming the foundations of my missionary work. Still, I must admit, there were both good and bad moments during our time in Chile.

The Lowest of Low Points

It was in Santiago that I experienced one of my lowest points as a missionary. Michele and I were struggling to assimilate into the language and cultural differences. I found driving challenging in the beginning. Santiago is blessed with one of the most elaborate subway systems in the world. The layout of Santiago, its roads, and the subway are all top-notch. But the driving… Oof. I invented these imaginary little guys I called the noggins. Often when I was stuck in traffic, the family joke was that the noggins would start to panic and run around on my head. As a result, I would be stressed to the point of wanting to pull my hair out.

On one such day, I was downtown in bumper-to-bumper traffic. No one was going anywhere. Then, a girl riding her bike through the cars scraped my beautiful Speed-the-Light[19] Hyundai Santa Fe. I couldn't believe it. She never stopped. I swung my door open to chase her when my door hit the car next to us, breaking off the car's rearview mirror. I said, "Wait here, I'll be right back." I chased down the girl on the bike and grabbed the back tire, and said, "Whoa! Do you know what you did?" She acted as if she didn't care. Words flew back and forth between us as all the surrounding cars enjoyed the entertainment. Here was this foreigner speaking in super-broken Spanish. People must have thought it was ridiculous.

But I wanted American justice. This American version of justice doesn't often work well in other countries. It is one of the main challenges that often destroys new missionaries or leads them to experience an internal (and inevitable) bitterness. You can't do missions thinking that American beliefs hold true throughout the rest of the world. Part of surviving on the mission field is learning to step out of your American self and become a citizen in a new country with a new culture and way of doing things. This is a tough lesson, but unless missionaries learn it and learn it well, they will probably never assimilate into their host country.

As a rookie in Chile, I didn't understand this thinking. I was still American in my thinking. At the same time, there was a country-wide promotional campaign dealing with domestic violence. What did it look like when a strange guy grabbed a bike tire, having a heated conversation with a girl with the whole world watching? Embarrassing.

I said, "Let's call the police." I took out my phone and suddenly realized I didn't know how to do it. So, I asked her how to call the police from my little pre-paid junk phone. That's when it dawned on me that I had crossed an invisible cultural line. I became what people refer to as the "ugly American." My actions showed my cultural ignorance, and the whole world knew it except for me.

I walked back to my car, talked to the man whose car mirror I broke, and we drove around the corner to the car dealership where he worked. He was test-driving a vehicle when I broke his mirror. I paid the dealer, climbed back in my car, and went home to retreat in my room and weep. It was as if all the cultural challenges I faced since arriving on the mission field came to a culmination that day. This incident broke something inside me. If you ever have the opportunity to live overseas with a foreign culture, you too may experience these moments we call *culture shock.* The Assemblies of God had tried to prepare us for these inevitable breakdowns back in orientation, but no book or classroom setting could have prepared me for what I felt that day.

Life is full of lessons. Serving God means you must recognize this fact and accept that these lessons never stop. We'll never be like Jesus completely. The challenge is to be on a constant mission of change while learning lessons. We must learn to apologize on some days, and on other days, we must learn to humble ourselves. We should also recognize that Jesus is for us. Peter walked on water with Jesus. It's safe to say no one else has ever experienced that moment. Yet, regardless of all he shared with Jesus, Peter had a continual growth process that was not easy for him.

First, he let Jesus down by denying Him—even after he said he wouldn't do such a thing. But somewhere along the way, despite his guilt, Peter remembered that Jesus was for him. Later on, we read in the book of Acts that Paul became enraged with Peter. Although Peter had received so much forgiveness, he had started to distance himself from eating with uncircumcised Gentiles because of the fear of criticism (Galatians 2:12). Jews considered Gentiles enemies of God. For a Jew, it was unthinkable to associate with anyone who wasn't circumcised. Whereas Peter initially ate with Gentile believers, he succumbed to the pressure of the culture which affected how he treated others. Galatians 2:11 tells us that Paul said of Peter, "I had to oppose him to his face."

God requires Christ-followers to grow. We can't follow Jesus and expect to stay stationary. It doesn't work. Hebrews 5:12-14 gives a clear indication that we have to mature and train.

> [12] You have been believers so long now that you ought to be teaching others. Instead, you need someone to teach you again the basic things about God's word. You are like babies who need milk and cannot eat solid food. [13] For someone who lives on milk is still an infant and doesn't know how to do what is right. [14] Solid food is for those who are mature, who through training have the skill to recognize the difference between right and wrong.

I pray that I don't have to experience a moment where God has to oppose me to my face because my actions are incoherent with the gospel message. Sadly, it's too easy to get into a comfortable groove where we fail to grow. In the Scriptures, we read that the Samaritans didn't readily accept Jesus. James and John said, "Lord, do you want us to call fire down from heaven to destroy them?" (Luke 9:54). At that moment, it was apparent that they lacked a sense of necessary spiritual maturity. Jesus "turned and rebuked them" (v. 55). He found it necessary to do what was required, speaking to them firmly to encourage them to grow and mature.

We don't know how God will deal with us, but if we're genuine in our efforts to follow Him, He will do whatever it takes to get ahold of us. It's up to us to open our ears and listen. James and John could have gotten mad at that rebuke; instead, they must have recognized that it was exactly what they needed. Maybe they even realized Jesus knew what they needed so they could grow.

FINANCIAL CRISIS

*When passion and discipline bring you to the brink of
your next divine opportunity, you still need the courage
to take the next step. There are times when that step
may seem like walking off the end of a diving board in
the dark. Yet, it is only through such acts of courage and
conviction that potential is translated into reality.*[20]

My first term was going fantastic. Pastors were reaching out, and I had the opportunity to minister all over the country. I got on buses headed to who knows where, only to be greeted at my destination by great people who would almost always invite me to stay in their homes. Whether I wanted to or not, I was learning Chilean culture. However, there were moments along the way when God wanted to teach me some lessons that only He knew I needed. One such lesson had to do with money. For those who are old enough to remember, 2008 was a trying year for many. The housing collapse that year led to severe financial hardships all over the United States. In my home state of New Jersey, the Wall Street turmoil impacted our churches all over the north of the state. Because many people from New Jersey worked in New York at the time, the financial crisis affected all of us. The ripple effect of the economic problems would soon reach us in Chile, not only us personally, but also at a country level.

As first-term missionaries, we had already lowered our budget to help us get to the field more quickly. Not only that, first terms are cut from four to three years so as not to over-stretch those limited budgets. Once a missionary gets beyond that first term, all successive missionary assignments typically last a minimum of four years. When we arrived in Chile, the exchange rate was about 570 pesos to one US dollar. At the worst of the American crisis, the exchange rate hovered around 450 pesos. Even without our landlord raising rent, the price went up nearly 28 percent. Food costs increased because of increased maritime shipping rates. Soon after that, the prices of goods rose to compensate for those same increases. That was the global impact of the crisis.

At a church level, people from New Jersey were losing their jobs. Churches were trying to weather the storm as our financial support began to wane. Many churches either suspended or stopped financially supporting us altogether. We asked, "God, what is going on?" This situation went on for months.

Living in Chile, we knew our kids depended on us to provide for them. I'll be honest; as a young missionary, I began to panic. When my monthly statement came in, I knew there was no way we could bear out the storm in a good way.

Slowly but surely, our financial cushioning started running out until it disappeared. I asked my mentor Mike what I could do. The struggle was real. We talked about putting a campaign together and phoning people. I was invited to speak at meetings and didn't want to go because I lacked the financial resources. There was often a cost to holding meetings at restaurants or other venues. It didn't matter if that cost was a little or a lot; I didn't have the money.

But God knew what I needed. Did I pray? You'd better believe it. Did I fast? Absolutely! Did I seek God? Every day. Did it work? In my humble opinion, no. Nothing was working. I was afraid for us, afraid for my kids, and as a dad, I felt like I wouldn't be able to provide for my kids. I wondered what would happen if the financial situation became so bad that the Assemblies of God would say, "Bob, we can't disburse any money to you this month because your account is empty." The Assemblies of God doesn't pay missionaries as salaried employees. The group is not responsible for making sure there's money to pay us. All missionaries have to raise their own support and respective budgets.

learn how to do future missions ministry.

Your Faith Will Be Tested

God knew He needed to test my faith. Could I trust Him during impossible times? These were questions I had to answer —me and me alone. God knew financial decisions would plague my future on when, where, and how to invest in missions, but He needed to be sure I realized my hope, strength, and sustenance came from Him. And so, if God calls me, He is ultimately responsible for providing.

Those words stung that day when I met with my area director in Argentina. Don had rejected my request and gave me some hard words. To be honest, I could have resented him. But here's the key, God doesn't always tell you what you want to hear! Read that sentence again. God doesn't always tell you what you want to hear! I'm intrigued by people who constantly seem to hear from God, yet He never says anything but good things to them. I'm not saying God is not using these people, but why does the God of the Bible, the example of a correcting God, speak only good words in our Christian circles? Think about that for a moment. Hard lessons and hard corrections have to prod us from time to time for us to mature. Does that mean we like it? Maybe not, but it's necessary.

While I didn't like my harsh correction, God again knew how to grab ahold of me. He didn't coddle me; He shook me! And I listened, and I learned. Thank you, Don, for those great words of wisdom, words I needed to hear: "Assemblies of God missionaries are faith missionaries." I went back home and did the only thing I could do, trust God. To my amazement, the economy did turn around. The exchange rate soon turned into 730 pesos to one US dollar! I ran to the bank as fast as I could and took out a bunch of money before it disappeared. When the time came to go home at the end of our term, we had more than $2,500 in our account. To God be the glory. I pray I never have to go around that mountain again, but I'll tell you this, it was a God-mountain. I had to hear God speak through Brother Exley; otherwise, I'd have paid the price long-term as a missionary. My faith, although real, wouldn't have been as rooted and as vibrant as it is today.

God Can be Trusted

The interesting thing about Chile is that the experience was necessary to prepare Michele and me for our God-designed future. I don't believe we would have ever had such a beautiful impact in Latin America without first serving in that country as Assembly of God missionaries. While I never understood God's purpose for sending us to Chile, it soon became crystal clear.

In my role as an evangelist, I frequently traveled through the country. For whatever reason, even despite my limited proficiency in Spanish, God opened church doors for us all over northern Chile. However, there was a catch. Doors don't open without people. Through my mentor, Mike, incredible doors were opened in the central and south parts of Chile. As a new missionary, I had no business speaking at the pastors' meetings in the Santiago section, yet Mike connected me with Superintendent Renee, who became a great friend. Superintendent Renee allowed me to speak to the Santiago pastors, and he opened the doors for me to speak at his church on occasion. I still have a copper Chilean keepsake hanging in my living room Renee gifted me. He recently went to be with the Lord, but Renee, I'll forever be grateful for your friendship. Because of our friendship, his son also became a friend. Through that friendship, I'd serve as the keynote speaker at Santiago's youth convention of over eight hundred young people. While Mike was instrumental in all of this, he wasn't my only missionary connection. Don Cartledge took me to the North with him to meet the crew from the Atacama Desert. That trip catapulted me into a season of ministry I'll never forget.

During that trip, I learned there were no missionaries serving the people there. The north desert was amazing with its dirt hills, the cold, the heat, and the people. No other missionaries were around, and the thought excited me. I thought, *I want to be here.* I knew I couldn't live there, but I could travel as God permitted. I made some incredible new friendships. The fact that these were Don's friends meant that they, too, were willing to be my friend because I was with him. That meant a lot. It was similar to my connection with the Espinoza-Marín family in Costa Rica. God put the right people in my life at the right time.

My missions journey would never have unfolded how it did if I had tried to do it alone. I needed people, but not just any people; I needed the right people. And thank God, He always allowed the right people to come into my life at the right time. If you can learn God's timing, you too will enjoy blessings beyond your wildest dreams. Don introduced me to David Muñoz, and from there, the rest is history. I went back to his church several times during my time in Chile, but there's one time I'll never forget.

I didn't have the money to go north. I was still in an economic shortfall caused by the housing collapse in the United States. In Chile, we had just experienced a magnitude eight-point-zero earthquake in the Tocopilla region, and I knew God was opening a door for us to do some spectacular outreach among the young people of the North. But I didn't have the money to travel. While I was praying one day, the Lord dropped some individual names in my heart. One of those names was my awesome boss from my computer days, who had supported us financially since we started. When I contacted him, he responded to my surprise with a generous check covering the trip's expenses. I was blown away. God provided as He has always faithfully done. God proved again—He can be trusted.

The day we arrived in the northern desert, it was unbearably hot. David picked me up at the airport and took me right to his house. I learned more about the event as we talked, but I also learned about the recent earthquake. Some of those kids sounded devastated, and they needed a touch from God. In reality, I was not ready for what God was about to do. It was a tremendous week that I pray I never forget.

During that week, God was moving. There was a sweet sense of the Holy Spirit at the place from day one. I preached with all of my being night after night. As a Pentecostal movement, the Assemblies of God believes that God is still active in the working of His Holy Spirit. We believe in the operation of the gifts Paul describes in his letter to the Corinthians. Many people experienced those gifts throughout the week. But the final night was special as it broke me. I finished sharing and played a video clip from the movie "The Passion of the Christ." At that moment, it was like the Holy Spirit broke free. Moving up and down the aisles, Jesus was becoming real to the kids seated there. Tears flowed from nearly every young person. All of a sudden, I sensed that God wanted to do more. They began to pray for one another intensely. Kids began to experience the baptism in the Holy Spirit with the evidence of speaking in other tongues. I was in shock. It was the first time I ever experienced anything like this in ministry. God was doing a work that went way beyond me as a person. I wasn't responsible for that move. I was only a tool in the hand of the Master. It was so much like the story of Peter. Peter shared a bold message in Acts 2, not because he sensed he had become someone, but rather because he sensed the Holy Spirit would take over and do what only God could do. That was me that night. I was in awe, but I believed that the Holy Spirit would achieve the purposes of God simply because I showed up and made myself available for God to use.

Once the youth conference ended, our family again loaded up and traveled to a place called Coquimbo. We were supposed to have another multiple-day youth conference in the northern part of the desert. This time, though, things turned out differently. I arrived with so much excitement about what God was going to do. I had just been part of a Holy Spirit move that I prayed would happen again. Maybe I tried to bottle up God's move, confining Him to a box through which I thought He needed to work. The first night I got up to share, it was as if I hit a brick wall. The experience that manifested itself in Arica was nowhere to be found in Coquimbo. Or maybe it did happen, but what I expected of God wasn't there. God moved during those few days, albeit in a totally different way. I left feeling somewhat discouraged. I felt that I had somehow missed the mark. Had I done something that chased God away? I was beating myself up over the outcome of that event. But why? It wasn't that the event was a failure; it was that my expectations fell short of what I wanted God to do. Just because God moves in one way in one place doesn't mean He will do the same everywhere. Maybe God changed His mojo because He knew I wanted to figure Him out. Maybe not. Who knows? But for whatever reason, God chose to minister differently to the kids in Arica and the kids in Coquimbo.

It wasn't until I returned to Santiago that things became clearer. There was a lesson for me to learn; I just didn't know it then. One evening I was driving with Don to the Bible school for a pastors' meeting when I said to him, "Don, I don't get why God seemed to disappear in Coquimbo. Do you think maybe I sinned or did something that separated me from His presence? Was I the reason for the difference?" On this occasion, God used Don to speak to me.

He said, "Bob, you're never responsible for the outcomes. You prepare, do your part, but when the rubber meets the road, God is responsible for the outcomes." So true. You can seek God intensely, you can pray until you're blue in the face, but sometimes, many times, God doesn't do what you expected Him to do. And you know why? He's responsible for the outcomes when we do our part. We can rest assured, there was a reason the Lord said the following in Isaiah 55:8-9:

> My thoughts are nothing like your thoughts," says the Lord. "And my ways are far beyond anything you could imagine. For as the heavens are higher than the earth, so my ways are higher than your ways and my thoughts higher than your thoughts.

Clearly, I needed to tuck that lesson in my heart. Ministry very rarely turns out the way you want. I can't tell you how many times I've stood before audiences only to have trouble connecting. That's the worst. What do you do when you get to the stage to deliver a message in forty-five minutes, and as you begin to speak, you feel like the people are ready to stone you? I've experienced situations like these many times. I will never forget one time.

I was visiting a children's center in Maipú in Santiago. Missionary Jim Mazurek was the founding pastor of this church. Jim is highly educated in the Bible and is known all over Latin America as a very reputable professor. It was quite humbling for me to be at his church. Who was I to be sharing at this amazing mission work behind the pulpit of this great preacher? I struggled through the message. By the time I finished delivering my message, I realized I had bombed big time. There was no response to the altar call. I waited for people to hurl stones in my direction. Instead, Michele came to the front on a prompting from the Lord and began to give an altar call with a short message tied into that call. The people responded immediately. I stood in awe. My wife, thank God, saved the day. Thank you, Michele, for being open to the voice of the Lord and responding to His prompting.

In my first term, I experienced many lessons like these. I still don't know why God took an individual like me, an unrefined type of man like Peter, and gently called me to follow Him when I was a teenager. I needed so much more growth and maturity to become the missionary God needed, a man full of wisdom that could only come by hearing the voice of the Holy Spirit.

Why did God choose me? Why am I a missionary and not some other person? Because God knew me, He knew where I'd stumble, fall, and fail, but when He chose to bring little Robertito (my nickname) into the world, He gave me an assignment that only I could choose to fulfill. It was no different with Peter. After many days of serious contemplation, maybe even incredible doubt whether he could ever be redeemed after what he did, Peter shows back up on the scene.

Passover came as it did every year. When Jesus experienced His final Passover, it was recorded in great detail, which would show us how painful it was for Him. As Jesus sat at His final Passover meal, He broke bread with His disciples, with whom He had shared many months, walking alongside them and living life. He knew the end was near. He then said, "One of you will betray me" (Matthew 26:21). Judas, who would soon be found guilty of betrayal, blurted out, "Surely you don't mean me, Rabbi?" (v. 25). The disciples couldn't believe Jesus would make such a bold statement.

Although we could discuss this story in more detail, let's focus on another aspect of Jesus's final moments. After that famous last supper, Jesus went to pray. He wasn't alone, for the Scriptures tell us He went with His disciples. But just before He spent time alone with God, He uttered distressing words. He said, "This very night you will all fall away on account of me" (Matthew 26:31).

The disciples couldn't believe what He was saying. Peter, Mr. Uneducated, Mr. No Tact, blurted out in his very impulsive way, "Jesus, you're crazy, how can I desert you! I've been by your side since I chose to follow you, and I'm not going anywhere." Perhaps Jesus found his reply a little humorous despite all that was going through His mind. He may have even smiled a little before saying, "Peter, you of all people, you are going to deny me three times" (Matthew 26:34). Peter vehemently denied it. "No way. Even if I have to die, I will not desert you" (v. 35). When the soldiers came to arrest Jesus, Peter pulled out a sword in his extreme fashion. Peter was a fighter; he was no highly educated super-elite. He was a blue-collar fisherman with no way of making history. He probably wouldn't fit very well in many of the upper-class circles of our day, yet Jesus chose him. Jesus told him, "You will deny me, not once, nor twice, but three times," yet He still chooses Peter.

Jesus likes to choose people through whom He can demonstrate His power. People with flaws, people with deficiencies that no finishing school could ever correct. He chooses the rich, the poor, the educated, the uneducated, and His reasoning is His alone. God chooses people who are careful to give Him glory. Paul tells us in 2 Corinthians 11:30, "If I must boast, I will boast of the things that show my weakness." Jump to chapter 12, and you'll read," My strength is made perfect in weakness" (v.8). Lastly, 1 Corinthians 1:27 lays it out clearly, "But God hath chosen the foolish things of the world to confound the wise; and God hath chosen the weak things of the world to confound the things which are mighty." God is a jealous God, and He chose Peter because He knew that at the end of the day, even when Peter stumbled, he'd stand up and give the glory to God.

The moment Jesus was arrested, the disciples had to struggle with what was taking place. Peter wasn't exempt from any of this. He, too, struggled with his faith and his pursuit of Jesus. When Jesus was finally put on trial, we see the man, Peter, come to the surface.

The Bible doesn't hold anything back or hide any harsh details. The writers of the Scriptures wanted us to know that the disciples were imperfect men following the one and only perfect man ever to walk the earth, Jesus. Peter, this bold soldier with the sword, was found to be sadly mistaken in his fidelity to Jesus when confronted about being with Jesus. He was asked multiple times if he was the disciple of the so-called criminal. In his account of the situation, Matthew made it clear that Peter emphatically denied Jesus (chapter 26). When the servant girls asked Peter about his connection to Jesus, he said, "I don't know what you're talking about" (v.70, 72, 74). And then it happened. "Immediately a rooster crowed" (v.74).

Sadly, Luke finally records that after Peter's third denial, "The Lord turned and looked straight at Peter. Then Peter remembered the word the Lord had spoken to him: 'Before the rooster crows today, you will disown me three times.' And he went outside and wept bitterly" (Luke 22:61-62). That moment must have crushed Peter. He knew he was guilty of doing what Jesus had mentioned. He had to eat his words.

Imagine if you were in a similar situation. How would you have responded, knowing that you betrayed your best friend? Peter claimed that he was ready to die for Jesus (Luke 22:33), but now when his best friend was at the worst point in his life, Peter cried out that he didn't know this Jesus. The guilt must have been unbearable.

In the case of Judas, who betrayed Jesus for money, the Bible says he found his guilt so overwhelming that he hung himself (Matthew 27:5). Imagine if Peter had done the same. The church as we know it would most likely not exist. Peter was crucial to the establishment of the current-day church. Jesus knew what would happen and how Peter would respond, yet He still chose to use Peter. Think about that. Before Jesus was nailed to the cross, He knew his best friend and confidant would deny him, yet He still chose Peter.

I pause to reflect on my own journey. Acts 2:22-24 says:

> Fellow Israelites, listen to this: Jesus of Nazareth was a man accredited by God to you by miracles, wonders and signs, which God did among you through him, as you yourselves know. 23 This man was handed over to you by God's deliberate plan and foreknowledge; and you, with the help of wicked men, put him to death by nailing him to the cross. 24 But God raised him from the dead, freeing him from the agony of death, because it was impossible for death to keep its hold on him.

These were Peter's returning words. He disappeared for a while, but when he came back, he came back with an incredibly powerful message. He wanted those who heard him to know that Jesus had to die. It was God's plan. I'm sure he was reminded of his guilt. Still, Peter lifted his head high and made it clear that even though people forced Jesus into an agonizing death, no power could hold Him. Jesus was and is alive.

Peter realized that God uses people to accomplish His will. He realized we all have an assignment. God will not force His bidding on anyone, but Peter knew he was responsible for his assignment. I love Peter because of the realness and relevance of his story. It connects with so many of our stories.

God was never afraid to hide the truth of the events surrounding the crucifixion. He needed us to know that first and foremost, Jesus died and rose again, and salvation belongs to us. God also wanted us to know that the only one who can disqualify us from experiencing salvation and fulfilling our assignment is us. He chose us. He chose you. He chose me. All I can say is God, thank you for letting me see the Peter you chose to use—the human Peter, the Peter who revealed that we're all broken, but still so very precious to God's heart and valuable to fulfilling our kingdom mission He has assigned.

Led By the Spirit

In a conversation with my neighbor one night, we talked about hearing God. I told him, "You know, the number one question I'm always asked is how do I hear God?" My neighbor, Paul, replied, "I believe it happens when we reflect." And later it dawned on me, yes, *He gets it*. Reflection, too, can be a powerful voice of God.

I loved it when J.D. Greear said:

> Being led by the Spirit is not an exact science. We shouldn't think of this process like a formula, and we should always approach this subject with an extreme amount of humility... I believe it is clear that God does move and speak in our spirits, but we must hold our certainty about his leadership with a little tenuousness, open to godly counsel, always subject to Scripture.[21]

The Word of God must always constrain our reflection, or we run the risk of stepping out of bounds. That night in the car with Don, I was able to reflect verbally, using him as a sounding board. More important than his advice was the wisdom he spoke using sound Bible doctrine. God used Don to open up the synergistic connections between myself and the northern Chileans. Remember, I had been excited when I first arrived in the desert and found no missionaries there. Something had said, "Here's where I want you." Whether Arica, Antofagsta, Tocopilla, Copiapó, Calama, the Atacama Desert was something special. I had known that was where I wanted to be. Even now as I reflect back on the events of those days, I remember how I was amazed one day at the move of God and discouraged the very next day because God didn't meet my expectations. In a Ford Aerostar on our way to a pastor's meeting, a moment of reflection prepared me to be sensitive to learn about how God moves. I was learning what Elijah had to learn in 1 Kings 19:11-13:

> The Lord said, "Go out and stand on the mountain in the presence of the Lord, for the Lord is about to pass by." Then a great and powerful wind tore the mountains apart and shattered the rocks before the Lord, but the Lord was not in the wind. After the wind there was an earthquake, but the Lord was not in the earthquake. After the earthquake came a fire, but the Lord was not in the fire. And after the fire came a gentle whisper. When Elijah heard it, he pulled his cloak over his face and went out and stood at the mouth of the cave. Then a voice said to him, "What are you doing here, Elijah?"

Elijah must have thought, *Surely God is in the wind*. No. Okay, surely God is in the earthquake or even the fire, but still no. God didn't come until the whisper. God was teaching Elijah that our expectations are not always what they seem. He is the one who chooses how He moves. Provided we do our part, He is responsible for the consequences. I learned that lesson that night as God spoke through His servant Don. I even began to discern that maybe God was up to something in the North. Maybe this feeling of "I have to be here" was more than a feeling. Maybe God prompted my wife that night when I bombed in Maipú. Without fully understanding why Arica seemed to go so well and Coquimbo so different, I began to think that ultimately, God was responsible for the outcome. I bombed in Maipú, but maybe there was a moral to the story. Maybe it was God's design for my wife to begin to trust her God-promptings as well. I'll never know the answer to most of these questions.

Michele and I continued ministering in the North even though we lived in Santiago. While it seemed slightly unorthodox to do so, I followed what I believed to be God's prompting in my spirit—the excitement and the desire to be in the desert north.

GOD'S TIMING

We need to become great, godly dreamers.[22]

After a fifteen-hour bus ride, having experienced my first Pullman sleeper bus, I finally arrived in the city of Antofagasta, Chile's second-largest city. The city is surrounded by an ocean on one side and by mountains on the other. These mountains separate Antofagasta from the vast desert. Coming into the city, you could see sirens mounted all over in the event that there was the imminent threat of a tsunami. Signs pointed to how to get out of the city in case of such an emergency. It was here that I met my new good friends, Leo and Edith. They had invited me for a week-long evangelistic crusade before I met them. We had connected through a series of mutual contacts, and I was finally there to minister in their church. I climbed off the bus, and just like that first time at the airport waiting to meet Mike, Leo was in the crowd looking for me. Since we had never met, he was probably looking for an out-of-place American that day. Somehow, we connected, and he took me back to his house.

Leo lived in a humble house that he probably built himself. Most of the houses in that area were somewhat pieced together. Some were made of cement, while others were made of sheets of *cin* (zinc in English). Leo told me that day, "I wasn't sure where to put you. We can't really afford to put you in a hotel, so I hope you're comfortable staying with us." I said, "Sure, I'd love to." He had his kids vacate their room; that would be my headquarters for the week.

Quite often when I traveled, I stayed with many pastors in their houses. It helped me speak Spanish twenty-four seven and provided a deep, intimate understanding of how Chileans lived their day-to-day lives.

When I first arrived in Antofagasta, I realized I was right thinking deserts were dry, hot, and barren, as one surmises from watching TV. While these descriptions are accurate, they don't give the full picture. Driving through the desert, one finds pockets of oases. There's greenery, lushness, and it's a wonder how such a thing can exist in the desert. Then there's the cold. In Calama, just outside of Antofagasta, the temperature can go down into the thirties. And believe me, one feels the cold in Antofagasta.

As the winds started to blow, the *cin* moved slightly back and forth, and the cold penetrated the room like the walls were made of mesh. I brought all my summer clothes because I never thought a desert would be cold. Television doesn't always give you the whole picture.

I can still remember shaking in my sleep during the evenings because I was so cold. I put on almost every piece of clothing I had brought to stay warm. However, no matter how much I put on, all I did was shiver. Trying to take a shower in the morning was another sign of my ignorance. The water was ice cold.

Looking around the neighborhood, one sees many houses with big black plastic reservoirs on top, which are used to hold water for the house. It generally doesn't rain in these parts of the world, and the Atacama Desert is known to be one of the driest deserts in the world.

Getting up after a cold night of shivering and trying to take a morning shower was a joke. Actually, I gave up on showering after a few days and used wet wipes to clean myself. After being there for some time, Leo finally told me they only showered in the evenings because the water is warmed up by then. Didn't I feel dumb?

Still, their family loved me as if they knew me all their lives. The refrigerator was barely stocked, and food items, including eggs, were bought daily. The only thing that really lived in the fridge was the "once" (pronounced in Spanish) tray with olives, cheese, avocado, ham, and a few other things—similar to an antipasto tray. This tray came out every day for tea-time, around five in the evening, and then went back in the refrigerator until the next day. Tea-time is a staple in almost every Chilean household. Still, whenever we sat down to eat, there was never a scarcity of food. Edith fed me extremely well. This couple and their kids treated me as if I were a longtime family member. They became great friends and will always be friends no matter where we go in the world.

The evangelistic crusades I experienced at their church were unbelievable. God showed up in unexpected, marvelous ways. One night, in particular, had a great impact on me as a minister. I had spent some time in prayer before going to church that third night, not realizing I was about to be God-thumped. Service started like normal, but the way it ended threw me for a loop. I was preaching about Moses and the burning bush that night. I used the wrong Spanish word, and someone from the congregation yelled out the right word. It was quite comical, and everyone chuckled. Some days, I said the wrong words, but the words I used aren't words you'd hear in church. Finally, at the end of the message, I launched into an altar call time. But this time, the temple lights went out. The sound system turned off, and I didn't know what to do. I was a little befuddled. *God, what's next?* I thought. Right about then, cell phones started lighting up all over. I thought, *Well, okay, we're doing this.*

With cell phone lights as our only light, we pushed into an altar time so that people could respond to Jesus. I tried to start with the youth. I say "tried" because it didn't end the way I had expected. When I called for the youth to come forward, everyone in the church came forward for prayer. "This is strange," I thought. "What happened to the youth?" But I wasn't going to abandon ship when people are responding. You keep pushing forward. So that's what I did. I discovered later that referring to the youth in a Spanish country meant anyone from age ten to fifty.

However, there was one more problem. Or, maybe I should say

I thought there was one more problem. In some churches, emotions dominate either the service or the altar time. Many times, when I gave an altar call for salvation, I never asked people to close their eyes and bow their heads. I believe those who respond to emotion may be less genuine than those who respond with a public confession of faith. As the evangelist preacher in that event, I was afraid the altar time was getting hijacked by emotional responses to God. Emotions are good, but I wanted people to experience God genuinely. Perhaps I was being more analytical instead of giving God total freedom to move.

As I began to pray for people up close, they began to drop to the floor. The Pentecostal realm calls this "being slain by the Spirit." I wasn't against what was happening but felt it was a programmed response to God. I thought, *Could it be that these people believe they have to fall on the floor when God touches them or when I get near them?* I was trying to be sensitive to the Holy Spirit while also wanting it to be a genuine move of God. I didn't want God to be reduced to an emotional experience or programmed response.

I stopped praying for people up close. Silently, I had a conversation with God, "God, I'm not going to pray for one more person up close. I don't want to be responsible for people falling. Lord, if they fall, I want it to be you—under Your divine power. I need You to move in this place, only You." I finished talking to God, moved up to the stage, and began to walk across the front of the church. I wasn't praying for anyone and kept a sizable distance on purpose. If something were to continue happening in that place, it needed to be a God-thing. Amazingly, as I walked across the platform, a wave of God's presence began to touch people from left to right. If I stopped, the wave appeared to stop; if I walked, the wave continued. Unable to explain what was taking place, all I can say is that I was amazed.

Here I was, trying to stop people from programmatically falling down, yet God still found a way to make it happen without me. It was incredible. I was trying to step aside for God to move, and He did. God didn't need me at all that evening. Yes, He used me to communicate His Word, but then the Holy Spirit took over from there. I don't know if I had struggled to believe in an active God who still worked through the power of His Holy Spirit, but I turned into a believer that night. I left the service, called my wife, and said, "Hon, you won't believe what happened. God was in that place."

That was my experience in Chile. Multiple God-moments with out-of-this-world times of ministry. Our time in Chile was unforgettable. My best friend to this day is a Chilean national, and we still communicate on an ongoing basis.

Still, there was an internal struggle within me. As much as I loved Chile, as much as I loved the incredible doors of ministry that God opened for us, I struggled to adapt to the Chilean cold and the unbearable Argentine-style nightlife. I was committed to the North; I had a church building project I was developing in Santiago, and let me be honest, the ministry was one million percent A-OK and awesome. But this small detail of the night culture was killing me. In Costa Rica, on the other hand, the sun came up early, the people got up early, and going to bed was generally at a reasonable hour. I began to struggle internally with the question: Once my first term finished, should I come back to Chile to complete our next four-year term, or is it wiser to change to another country where we can fit in both ministerially and culturally? Michele was finally plugged into ministry working at an all-girls orphanage, and our kids had their friends. Life was simply good. I was afraid to change all that, but I was also afraid that I'd never be able to adjust to the cold and the nightlife.

Knowing that time was running short, I went on an intentional search for God to tell me what to do. I wanted him to tell me, "Stay in Chile, or go to XYZ country." I had many conversations with Michele. Even though my kids were young, we engaged them in the conversation. We've never made a major family decision without in some way involving the kids in that process. We're a family, and I'm not going to drag my kids all over the world without getting their input. Sometimes decisions are made when they don't agree, but as a family, I needed them to be involved.

I printed out a map and posted it on my wall so I could pray specifically about alternate countries. Michele and I had a list of the advantages and disadvantages of leaving Chile. This decision weighed heavily on us, especially because it affected not only me and Michele, but also the kids. We tried to use every strategic decision process available while still always seeking God.

In prayer one morning, I sensed God saying, "Costa Rica." Immediately, I thought it was me. "God, this can't be you. Remember? Michele, in my conversations with her, was adamant that when we left Costa Rica, she did not want to return there in a missionary role." I told God, "Michele feels very uncomfortable with certain aspects of life there. So, God, here's the deal, I'll pray about it, but she needs to say to me that she feels you leading us there." It seemed to make sense that if God were going to open that particular door, He had to talk to my wife. While I felt this tug in my heart toward Costa Rica, the prayer map didn't reflect that tug. In fact, I tried to twist God's arm. I wanted to convince Him there may be two other countries He might consider. The first was Panama, and the second was Honduras. I guess I was trying to make a deal with Him.

Up until this point, I had told no one about this family decision we were agonizing over. When we finally did have a conversation with our regional director about our concerns on returning to Chile, I received a phone call from the area director for Central America. I still had not mentioned Costa Rica to Michele nor anyone else. Costa Rica was top-secret between God and me. I brought up that we might be considering a transfer to Panama or Honduras because I had already been told Cuba wasn't going to happen back when I initially applied as a missionary. I made sure that Cuba was never part of this transfer request. I still remember that when I first talked to my regional director about a potential move to Central America, he told me, "If you want to make this move to get closer to Cuba, forget about it." He did not say that because I brought it up; rather because he knew I had originally applied for Cuba.

After a lengthy conversation with the Central America area director, he didn't think we'd be a good fit for Panama nor Honduras. Then he name-dropped a country that made my heart explode. "What about Costa Rica? You had great national friends there. You fit in well with the Costa Rican people, and Michele's work with girls would translate well into that country." Again, I had said nothing about my top-secret God-tug. We had a great conversation, agreed to pray about it, and we left it there until...

Let's pause a moment and unpack an important life lesson. When you're truly following God's will and not constantly sitting idle, you don't have to kick down doors to force God's will. If you try to force God's will, you can end up destroying what God has planned for you. It's all about timing—God's timing. I could have pressured Michele or tried to make my own path to Cuba, but I'd have destroyed my missionary assignment and God's fullest blessings on the ministry.

I pleaded my case before God, but God wasn't sending what I felt was the right kind of provision. Panicking, I sent an email to my boss Dick at Assemblies of God Missions. I said, "Dick, things are really bad financially. I only have six months left on this first three-year term; can we return to the United States before we're out of money?" His response was to involve my area director, Don Exley, who lived in Argentina. Already having a trip scheduled to Argentina, I asked my area director if we could meet, and he agreed. I thought they were going to let us go home to do some more fundraising. Was I ever mistaken! Don let me know he was quite perturbed with me because I sent the request to the top without involving him in the conversation. Unintentionally, I had sidestepped the chain of command, which is the biggest no-no ever. Don gave me a mini-lecture and then confronted me, saying, "You know that Assemblies of God missionaries are faith missionaries. Your request has been denied."

My heart dropped to the floor. Now, what am I going to do? I honestly had no idea. These weren't the words I wanted to hear, but these were the words I needed to hear. These were God's words to me. I needed to step back and step out of my situation for a minute to hear them.

I had always tithed, even as a teenager. As a young man, I had told my wife, "Hon, I want God to bless me." I did whatever it took to position myself to be able to receive from God. I didn't struggle in my giving. I had left my career; I had sold my house; I had even moved in with my parents for a season. I was willing to make sacrifices—but this situation? "God, I think you might be going a little far this time." I had always been faithful with my money in giving. I believed that every penny I had ever earned came from God. That meant there was no question about giving ten percent tithe, plus any offerings, and trusting God. But was I really trusting God? If I were panicking and trying to fix the situation on my own, did I really believe that God would provide for us? Did I believe that God had created the pathway for me to be in Chile? If I truly trusted God, I needed to wrestle with the idea that He would provide for us. I had to learn these life lessons to

tor, I can't guarantee you that I'll be coming back to Chile, but if we do, I'll commit to helping you build your church building on the land that you purchased." This offer wasn't a spur-of-the-moment decision. I had been building a friendship with Hector for many months, and I was honestly ready to take the next step with him in building God's kingdom. Hector was thrilled. He had a vision packet already prepared of what he wanted to do and how he wanted to build the church. I needed to make sure there were no misunderstandings about my commitment. I had him sign a document stating that he understood I'd help him build a church if we returned to Chile. However, if God opened another door, I'd not be coming back.

I wasn't shutting the door for God in Chile. Our ministry wasn't formally over there, and I lived like nothing was going to change. Still, I set realistic expectations at the same time so that there were no surprises for anyone. I had to continue pushing ahead, following God. If I were to come back, I wanted to make sure I was ready to hit the ground running. On the other hand, if I didn't return, I didn't want to disappoint Hector because I abandoned him. Ultimately, our first term was coming to an end, and we'd be returning to the United States for our next twelve months of fundraising. However, when the day came, and we did return to the States, we had no more clarity for our next assignment on the missions field than before. So, I continued to preach with all my heart, believing that we'd return to Chile to build Hector's church right next to the national stadium.

Special God-Moments

Early on in our next fundraising cycle, I discovered that a compassion forum would be held in Springfield, sponsored by the Assemblies of God. Immediately, I thought of Michele. While in Chile, she ministered to young girls at an orphanage. I reasoned that this forum would be the ideal resource to get her more tools to make her more effective.

"I'm not going alone," she said.

"For Pete's sake, can I get a win here?" I thought. "Both of us can't go," I said. "I have to fundraise, but you can go."

So finally, I convinced her, and she went. This God-moment changed our lives. At that conference, she met Beth Grant, founder of Project Rescue. Michele talked with her, spoke with the people at the conference, and she, too, had conversations with God. She felt a God-tug on her heart. She felt the call and was challenged to respond to the opportunity in Costa Rica for ministering to ladies and girls impacted by human trafficking. She tried to shake it off, but the tug only grew stronger. God, in His way, broke her down at that conference because she was willing to make herself sensitive to His voice and call.

God often speaks, and yet we never hear Him. The reason is that we don't allow ourselves to be sensitive enough. If we don't position ourselves in the right environments or have conversations with God and wait for Him to speak through prayer or His word, we may never hear Him. But because Michele was sensitive to God's voice at the conference that day, the Lord was able to nudge her toward a new ministry in Costa Rica, even though she wasn't thinking about it.

When she returned from Springfield, Michele said, "Hon, let's do it. I trust you as the spiritual leader of our home. If you feel like Costa Rica is where God is leading us, let's do it."

I wanted to scream for joy. I said, "Hon, that's what God laid in my heart months ago. I didn't want to tell you until you had your God-moment."

It's all in God's timing. He spoke in a soft whisper in my heart, and I had to be sensitive enough to be aware of the tug toward Costa Rica, but then I had to wait for God to work the rest out. The moment Michele came to me, it was official. God intervened at that very moment, setting us on a course for Costa Rica.

But wait, there's more! Part of the reason the area director of Central America mentioned Costa Rica was because he thought Michele's ministry with girls would translate well there. As a matter of fact, the Costa Rican Assemblies of God had never done anything to intentionally address human trafficking, sexual exploitation, or prostitution. It was a known problem, especially given the large number of male tourists visiting the country. Michele had struggled with the sexualization of women when we were there the first time. Still, at the same time, God was tugging at her heart toward ministering to these ladies. When Jay brought up her ministry and how it could fit in Costa Rica, he hit a chord. She knew that it was time. She knew God's timing caught up to her, and He was opening a door for her to minister with her God-given gifts.

That phone call about ministering in Costa Rica had to go through an incubation phase that didn't develop until that meeting with Beth Grant. Soon after, an invitation from the Costa Rican superintendent opened the door for us to come. We'd help develop the church and a act as the catalysts for a grassroots initiative, focusing on ministering to ladies trapped in human trafficking.

With our country assignment settled, I was left with a new challenge. What started as Chile was now going to be Costa Rica. How was I going to tell Hector in Santiago? That conversation was going to be complicated, even though it wouldn't surprise him. It still doesn't make it any easier to tell your friend that you're now not going to help him build his church.

One day he reached out to me. "Roberto, we were talking about you at the executive committee, and I wanted to find out how things are going."

"Lord, help me," I thought. I broke the news, and naturally, he was sad, maybe even discouraged. They had wanted to build for so long in a marginalized area, but they couldn't afford it. Should I have ever offered to help him build his church? I've struggled with that question for years. Did I do the right thing by having that discussion with him? Even after all this time, I still find it difficult thinking back to that phone conversation. I loved Hector dearly. He continues to reach his community in a fantastic manner.

Maybe you sense a God-tug on your heart. Maybe He's saying to you, "It's your time." You may not be a missionary overseas, but can you finance the construction of a church temple. You can make a difference around the world in countries like Chile when you get behind overseas missionaries in the form of prayer and finances. Perhaps God is prompting you to pray for Hector. That's a great place to start. You can accomplish many awesome things through prayer. Position yourself to be sensitive to God; you'll be surprised how much He has to say.

HERE WE COME TIQUICIA (COSTA RICA)

*Know which part of the Lord's work He has called you
to and give your whole soul to it. —Charles Spurgeon*

It was said of Lincoln that his leadership style was highly connected to his "finely developed sense of timing—knowing when to wait and when to act."[24]

Timing would become very clear for us during this stage of ministry. Throughout our missionary career, we had so many unanswered questions and so many challenges, but I often failed to understand why God worked out the timing the way he did. Cuba was still nowhere on the radar. I told everyone God was preparing work for us in Cuba. Sometimes, I still questioned whether I made a mistake in hearing or thinking God had planned Cuba for me. People must have honestly thought I was out of my mind. Ever since I was a kid, I was emphatic in my belief that we'd be missionaries in Cuba, yet the circumstances dictated that I might have been mistaken.

Arriving back in Costa Rica, only two other missionary families were working on the ground at the time. One family had been there for nearly two years, and the other family had arrived only a few days before us. In other words, there weren't any troops waiting for us to arrive in the country. From the day we arrived, we were on our own. We had to figure out where to live, how to get a car, and all the other things you need to do to set up a house.

These are very good experiences. In doing so, a missionary learns the ins and outs of the local culture. In the United States, people looking for a house usually find a real estate agent, and the agent does most of the work in finding a home for them. On the other hand, in Costa Rica, it's always possible to hire an agent, but you miss out on a whole segment of real estate. I'm referring to the real estate not listed in the formal market. If you're only looking for American-style housing with American-style prices, you'll severely limit your options. It's much better and wiser to get in a car and drive all over town.

My Costa Rican family was still there, and they were our first point of contact. Dyhana and her fiancée picked us up and drove us all over the city looking for a place to live. We finally found a great condo that we loved, and in the process, we cultivated a priceless friendship!

Our God Mission

Once we were all set up, it was time to start our ministry. We never forgot why we came back to Costa Rica. We were committed to our mission of "giving girls back their childhood and giving communities churches with purpose." What a huge mission. It was, for us, a God mission. We needed God.

First of all, we recognized we could never erase the past of those ravaged by human trafficking situations. Any form of sexual abuse is horrendous. People are left with scars that take years to heal. Have you ever heard it reported that you could rescue a human trafficking victim for fifty or a hundred dollars? Once I heard an organization make such a claim. Impossible. I repeat, it's impossible to rescue and restore a girl for fifty or a hundred dollars. It takes thousands of dollars. It takes many, many hours of counseling. It takes time, and lots of it. It also takes consistency on the part of the organization dedicated to intervening in these situations.

During a prayer session, I sensed God speaking, telling me to give these girls back their childhood. That meant using the environment of play to minister restoration. Think how many of these girls have never had a childhood because of the sexual abuse they experienced. Think about the fact that some of them never had Barbies or dolls; they never knew what it meant to play as little girls.

God had given me two daughters. Up until that prayer session, I didn't understand why. God gave me my two daughters because He knew He needed to soften me; that's a fact. Before Michele was pregnant with Isabella, our second daughter, I told her, "Michele, I'm ready for another child. I think I want another little girl."

I fell in love with my kids. And whenever they went outside or went over to their friends' houses, I repeatedly asked them, "Girls, what's your job today?" And their reply had to be, "Have fun." I wanted them to be little girls, to play, to have fun. And so naturally, that spilled over into ministry.

Where do you think you excel at ministry? Look at your life. Where have you naturally excelled? What are your natural inclinations? These are key to what God has in mind for you in ministry. An incredible life lesson here involves understanding that God doesn't pull your ministry out of a hat. He prepares you throughout your life! Take a hard look at your life. Take inventory. You'll find out precisely what he has planned for you.

For me, even as a kid, I was always intentionally different. I wasn't satisfied with fitting in with the crowd. It may have made my life a lot harder than it needed to be. But it was important for me to be different, and I liked to do things people said were impossible to do. So, when I looked for a ministry, I discovered that I liked going to the most challenging places and the most difficult people. When I worked with pastors, I enjoyed mining for the beauty in the underdog. I found it gratifying to see the beauty that could come from the ashes. If I had chosen the easy places, I'd have missed what God had in store for me.

Giving Girls Back Their Childhood

Whenever we were engaged in a ministry event, such as a morning or single-day retreat, we always incorporated our mission of giving girls back their childhood. "Girls" was a term we chose to encompass all our female beneficiaries from ages twelve and older. Michele co-directed a weekly youth group of over fifty teens, and boys and girls could attend the group. Some of these kids were in situations involving sexual exploitation; others had moms working in the sex trade, while others were what we called at-risk youth. These kids ranged from twelve to eighteen years of age. The at-risk youth came from impoverished neighborhoods where any hope of a future outside of prostitution seemed unlikely. The older beneficiaries were women who fell into the over-eighteen age category. They all came throughout the week. These ladies were broken up into small group settings. Each group received individualized attention during an intentional two-year restoration process, which included holistic care and vocational training.

Everything we did had to involve creating childhood experiences of play. Our mission had a non-negotiable quality that kept us focused on how we ministered restoration. Also, the idea of "giving girls back their childhood while helping them discover what it meant to be a follower of Jesus Christ" was central to our mission. We can't disconnect ministry from the main idea of Jesus. The gospel of Christ is the reason we do anything related to ministry. Take Him out of the equation, and we're just left with a social initiative. There's nothing wrong with social initiatives, and I applaud those engaged in worldwide social efforts. Even though it's possible to have impactful, beneficial initiatives without the Jesus-component, these initiatives will lack God's supernatural power—power for provision, power for change, but most importantly, the power to affect eternity. Jesus never said, "I will build social organizations...," he said, "I will build my church and the gates of hell will not prevail against it" (Matthew 16:18).

Giving girls back their childhood wasn't enough! They also needed to learn what it meant to follow Jesus. This missional focus was our true north. It would keep us on the right path pursuing what we deemed to be our God-goals.

Michele and I realized from the beginning that we couldn't

do it alone. Involving people was key to the success we all had envisioned. Many anti-trafficking organizations throughout the world emphasize the importance of teamwork. The Australian Government recently summarized the need for teamwork when it said:

> We must work together in close partnership to combat modern slavery. It is only through our joint efforts that we can develop and implement a holistic response to modern slavery in Australia. This is why we will collaborate across government and with international partners, civil society, business, unions and academia to ensure a coordinated response to modern slavery.[25]

Human trafficking has been an issue for centuries. The Apostle Paul addressed the issue of sexual prostitution in 1 Corinthians 6. If sexual abuses have been around since the beginning of time, one person could never hope to eradicate this issue. People working together is effective, but not just any people: they must be Spirit-led people. It's easy for resentment or bitterness to grow when you work closely with others. Working with people takes patience; it takes Spirit-led hearts to form bonds of unity.

Michele and I recognized these facts from the beginning. We discussed how we'd find people who could address the crimes of human trafficking in Costa Rica. Since we were foreigners, we had to find the right players. If we were going to make a difference, we needed connections to do our job well. If, for some reason, we had to suddenly leave Costa Rica, we wanted our ministry work to continue uninterrupted. However, if we could form strategic local alliances, we could invest in a local-run legacy that would endure for a long time.

The search went on for months until we discovered an organization that seemed to be one of the major players in this area of need. As an additional plus, this organization was faith-based. We started phoning, but had no success—no callbacks. After all these years, I now understand why. Human trafficking is a buzzword today. People from all over are opening their eyes to the plight of women worldwide. Governments from every continent have started to recognize the issue. But many people want to become involved for the wrong reasons. Some people have experienced sexual abuse, while others have a scarred childhood —both mentally and physically. Human trafficking, genital mutilations, and horrific crimes way beyond our comprehension bombard the news. Migrants from all over the world are trying to make their way to the United States with the hope of a better future. We hear of drug cartels, children being trafficked through the desert for large sums of money, and unthinkable accounts of women and girls being raped during their journeys. It's difficult to imagine what these journeys entail. While carrying out research for my Ph.D. thesis, I read many women's stories of being smuggled into neighboring countries. They were then forced to work as sex slaves to repay the smuggler's debt that had compounded over the many days, weeks, or months of their journeys. The news rarely reports these types of stories, but they happen.

Many people want to become involved and help those affected by sex crimes. Sadly, few understand the commitment, the consistency needed, or the pains endured by those addressing these crimes on the front lines. Organizations must be cautious about who they let into their circle of influence. Cartel thugs and traffickers might be trying to infiltrate the organization to stop its effectiveness. Again, that's why it's crucial to have Spirit-led leaders.

It felt like this faith-based organization in Costa Rica was stonewalling us. But that's the beauty of working with God. You have to work, you have to move, but it's not your job to force His will. He will do what He needs to do—at His own time. One day we called again, and by chance, they answered. Later, they invited us to come in for an in-person conversation.

The day of that meeting at the organization's headquarters proved to be a God-ordained, timely, and miraculous encounter. Michele and I were talking in the coordinator's office when Raquel, the founder, overheard our voices. She perceived us to be a young couple with an underdeveloped Chilean accent, but Chilean nonetheless. She walked down to meet us and asked, "Who are you, and why do you have a Chilean accent?" We explained that we were Assemblies of God missionaries and that we had recently transferred from Chile to Costa Rica. Michele talked about her past, her work in the girls' orphanage, and our missional reason for being in Costa Rica. I shared briefly about my role as an evangelist in Chile. I also discussed how God had opened doors for us to work in the northern Atacama region with the churches in Arica, Antofagasta, and Copiapó.

Standing there with the biggest grin, Raquel says, "I'm from Chile. Not only that, but I'm also from the northern Atacama region."

No way! I thought. We both looked at each other in disbelief. Could it be that God was preparing us for this day all along? We were shocked but interested to see how this situation would continue to unfold.

"Are you kidding us?" we asked.

"I was over at the Swedish embassy, and for some reason, I felt like I needed to get back here. I wasn't even supposed to be here today, and then I heard your accent. It intrigued me. That's why I came to meet you," said Raquel.

We learned that she emigrated to Costa Rica as a young lady. She had an encounter with Jesus through watching the Christian Broadcasting Network. Because of a dream she had, this woman followed God and founded a place that could minister to women who experienced sexual abuse, prostitution, and human trafficking.

It was as if God said to us that day, "Now you know why you had to go to Chile. Now you know why I opened and shut certain doors. If you had never been to Chile, this moment would have never been possible."

It caused me to pause and thank God for His divine guidance, even when we weren't always aware of it. Follow the timeline of events:

1) We helped to plant a Spanish church in the United States where one of our attending friends was Costa Rican

2) His family becomes our family when we get to Costa Rica

3) We move on to Chile, where my evangelist role (that wasn't supposed to happen) allowed me to minister in the North

4) We are transferred to Costa Rica in part because of our story, Michele's ministry, and our pseudo-family in Costa Rica

5) We finally develop a friendship with a Chilean lady who worked in trafficking and made her home in Costa Rica.

No one could pay to make these kinds of things happen. If it were not for the providence of God and keeping my ear keenly aware of the Holy Spirit's inaudible voice, we'd have never experienced what Jesus calls living life to the fullest (John 10:10). We were truly living a life of abundance that went beyond financial prosperity. I have been thanking God for that day ever since. We became great friends with this lady over the next eight years. Michele and I had two very separate roles in working with this organization and the women involved.

As a man, I needed to distance myself from any interactions with the ladies who fell into the over-eighteen category. Their prostitution "jobs" required them to be seductive, and they dressed and acted accordingly. It would have been unhealthy for me to have any direct involvement with them. For that reason, I worked on tasks unrelated to women, such as computer work, administrative duties, or staff discipling.

Michele was engaged in sting operations. Once the women were rescued or apprehended, she'd frequently share her life story with ladies in the brothels. While she was never a victim of human trafficking, Michele always found a way to connect with the ladies on a personal level. As the connection point, she helped them discover and experience Jesus.

Consistency

We had raised the necessary funds so we could invest in programs that would serve this population. Our missional strategy served us well in the beginning. We decided early on that we'd only invest in events designed around childhood play. In addition, there had to be an opportunity for these women to discover what it meant to be a follower of Jesus Christ. In one event, the ladies took a one-day trip to nearby pools. We never scheduled trips longer than one day because many of the women still worked as prostitutes. Some worked alone, and others had pimps, and some were involved in human trafficking situations. It was hard to distinguish who was in what kind of situation. Our interactions were based on trust, and the more trust we developed, the more they opened up.

During the trip to the pool, we focused on the shallow end of the pool. Michele was one of the first to jump in. She was just as rowdy as everyone else, if not more. When she got out, a psychologist on staff told her, "Michele, you can't be in the pool playing with those ladies. You must maintain professionalism. You have to show that you're different."

Michele was heated. And she had every reason to be so. We had already determined that our ministry to these ladies was to give them back their childhood and help them discover what it meant to have a relationship with Jesus Christ. You can't achieve this purpose without being in the trenches with them. Michele knew it. And she was true to her mission of creating those environments of childhood play. Every event didn't have to be the same, but if we were to be involved, they had to be missional and consistent.

Unless your commitment follows a pattern of ongoing consistency, you'll never find the key that unlocks the inner chambers of most of these precious hearts affected by human trafficking. These women never know who to trust because all they have ever known is deceit and corruption. Our prayer each morning is that God will always open the right doors for us to touch the right hearts at the right time.

Relationships Require Work

From that first day of meeting members of the organization, God joined our paths because of divine encounters. We never had to kick one door open. We had to be sensitive, listen to His voice, and be ready to move, but if we had tried to kick, I guarantee you, this book would never have been written. It's amazing how we went from having no contacts and no knowledge of trafficking in Costa Rica to an encounter with a Chilean who unlocked the door to a beautiful, although rocky future.

Rocky future? We started with the most amazing story of divine opportunity. It seemed almost perfect, so how could it become rocky? Honeymoons are great. They often come with surprises, newness, and shared experiences. God is all for honeymoons. God loves for us to have mountaintop experiences.

When I married Michele, we had the most exciting honeymoon in Jamaica. We still tell stories of the unforgettable experiences we shared as a newlywed couple. Once we came back home, we had to learn to live together. Here's my advice if you're married. You could be one, twenty, or even thirty years into marriage, but the most challenging thing in a marriage is melding your pasts. Both husband and wife have different pasts, which means lots of opportunities for conflict and rocky roads. Both have to learn to live with one another through the good and the bad.

Ministry and church life are no different because they can't happen without people. It's impossible to engage in the work of the church where different life paths don't cross. In those crossings, everyone needs to learn to do life together. Jesus knew this would happen because He knows people. He knows we all have different pasts, areas which dictate how we'll work together. And in knowing all of this, He told His closest friends, "My children... love one another" (John 13:33-34). The only way any ministry or relationship works is if you love one another.

Even in America, we come from different cultures. Americans from New Jersey are not like South Carolina Americans. We're just different. And that's how it must have been with Jesus's disciples who all came from different places, different experiences. So as He was about to make His way to the cross, Jesus told them, "love one another" (John 13:34). He knew it would be challenging but necessary. Jesus was no exemption. In John's book, we read that Nathanael the Israelite asked about Jesus, "Can anything good come from Nazareth" (John 1:46). Nathanael judged him because of his origins, his differences. Yet Jesus had to determine in His heart to love, to look beyond differences.

When I started working with this organization as our partner organization in Costa Rica, God had divinely set up the opportunities, but that didn't erase the past. I had to overcome patterns set by other missionaries at other times. Raquel and even the staff had personal experiences with Americans who colored their view of foreign missionaries. On one occasion, Raquel told us, "Roberto, Michele, if you had not been missionaries in my home country in my town, I'd have never worked with the two of you." God knew. God knew what we needed, but that still couldn't and wouldn't erase the past.

Previous relationships with other donors left the impression with our partner organization that every time a financial need presented itself, there was an obligation for the donor to fund that need. Subsequently, there was always a financial urgency, always a need. The very fact that Michele and I were constrained by a missional focus soon created tensions between us and this organization. We weren't there to give to anything and everything. We were there to give girls back their childhood while they discovered what it meant to become a follower of Jesus Christ. Even though there were good initiatives that needed funding, we weren't the answer.

While this created unfortunate tensions, we still pushed ahead. We had four phenomenal years in Costa Rica. The doors God opened were out-of-this-world miraculous. The organization with which we partnered had a Christ-centered focus, a mission with which we could work, and together, there were some great individuals we were able to impact with the message of Jesus Christ.

Those first four years wound down quickly. To this day, I continue to stand in awe at how God prepared our paths to cross in Costa Rica. The successes that God gave us during those years were unforgettable. Raquel spent twenty-plus years building a dream God gave her. When we arrived, she had already done the hard work of tilling the soil, preparing hearts, and completely investing herself. We were truly able to stand on her shoulders and run with something into which she poured her blood, sweat, and tears. I'll never understand the sacrifices she made to create this vision from God. She was a woman in Central America pioneering a one-of-a-kind organization in the country—this lady was exceptional. She wasn't only attempting but doing great things for God and people.

All In

Michele will never forget those final sting operations she, Raquel, and our partner organization's psychologist staff participated in just before we returned to the United States.

They went out one evening with the police, Interpol, the immigration department, and everyone involved in the sting operation. Someone had previously informed the police that they saw underage girls in a local nightclub. It was a long night with many interviews, but by the end of the night, no one was any closer to finding the minors that were suspected to be present. On their way out of the door, an officer began to yell for help. He had discovered an underage girl hidden beneath the stage of the nightclub. She had been stashed away so that no one could discover her. That young girls discovery was a success, but I can assure you it was a painful one. You don't find underage girls hidden beneath stages and expect not to have some sort of post-traumatic response. When you discover that this kind of nightlife exists right under your nose, you hurt for those that are still out there. The burden you carry for helping other unidentified victims intensifies within you.

This case wasn't an isolated incident. In the newspaper, reports surfaced about luxury prostitution rings, corrupt mayors using their political power as a means to exploit young people sexually, and the list goes on. Listening to these stories as a counselor eats away at you. Working to create change comes at a price. Your emotional well-being will often be challenged. Working in this area of ministry is not for everyone. It's especially not for those who only want the T-shirt that says, "I've been involved in helping rescue and restore those impacted by human trafficking." I firmly believe that those involved in this area of church ministry need a unique and divine call from God. The call is a reminder of the mission God has given you and why you're there.

In God's unexpected way, I was recently in a church service where He used the fundraising of a pastor to challenge me. The pastor was raising funds to replace broken chairs in the sanctuary. He stated, "I'm buying twenty-five chairs myself," and then he used three words that struck a chord in my spirit. He said, "I'm all in." While this quote seems so random, God used it to challenge me towards my call with Him. I had to ask myself, "Am I all in for God?"

How many of us are all in for what God has for us? Don't expect it to be easy. Expect that there will be obstacles of every kind. But all in wins confidence. All in unlocks people's hearts. All in gives God the best chance in the world at using you to your full potentiality.

Our story, one of many divine encounters, constantly reminded us of why we were there. It wasn't because we thought it would be cool to invest ourselves into ministering restoration to those impacted by sexual abuse crimes. It was because God called us, God set us up as a couple, and he made all the connections. We became like that pastor with the chairs, "all in."

LIFE HAS PURPOSE

Fire tests the purity of silver and gold but the
Lord tests the heart — Proverbs 17:3

Four years into our first term in Costa Rica, we again had to close up shop to return to the United States for our next twelve-month fundraising cycle. This time it was a little different. We knew that we were going back to Costa Rica. What's more is that before leaving Costa Rica, the partner organization with which we had been working received an incredible blessing from God. They had received finances to buy an expensive property to build a shelter for human trafficking victims.

Michele and I were very much on board! We recognized this would be a place where the ladies could live and experience restoration, while becoming immersed in a Christ-centered atmosphere. Not only did we envision a safe place for restoration, but also a church home for the ladies living there. We were excited.

The land was well-removed from the capital of San Jose, but at the same time still accessible, although only by 4x4 vehicles. We compiled a formalized working relationship between this organization and the Assemblies of God during our final days in country so that we could be a part of building this place of restoration. However, if we were going to help build, we had to protect our investment. I needed to ensure that any and every dollar raised for the construction of this amazing shelter would be channeled in its entirety to the shelter.

I sat down with my pastor in Costa Rica, and we talked at length about the project. There was no way I'd do anything without the Costa Rican Assemblies of God blessing. He warned me

THE COMPASSION FORUM

Pursuit of God is a regular confession of our absolute need
of him. In turn, we open ourselves to His examination
at the point of our greatest vulnerability.[23]

With Michele's permission, I'll share her side of the story. Ending that phone call, Michele wasn't in agreement. You could see her shaking her head in dismay. She was dead set against going to Costa Rica. That was one area where she wasn't going to budge. I didn't know how to handle this.

For married couples, there has to be a back-and-forth trust; there must be a constant give and take. Moving our family to another country was a big deal. I knew I couldn't force the situation if God were to have His way. Still, I wasn't stopped dead in my tracts. Our missionary assignment wasn't over. I wasn't sure what the future would hold. Neither was I finished with Chile. We were still living there, engaged in ministry, and it was always possible we'd return there as missionaries. Yet, I had this uneasiness on the inside that told me I'd never be able to adapt to the cold and Chilean nightlife. The decision was ripping my insides apart. The decision to leave Chile was hard beyond words.

Since my wife had her feet firmly on the breaks, I didn't know what the future held. I did the only thing I could: I embraced the present. I continued to follow God in my current assignment, believing that He would work out our futures without me making it happen.

I met with a pastor in Santiago, a good brother and close friend by the name of Hector Areyvalo. He was a businessman turned pastor within the Assemblies of God. I told him, "Hec-

of certain pitfalls, especially those related to Costa Rican law. Afterwards, he said, "Always know, I'll support you all the way." For me, that sealed the deal to the beginning of a newly built relationship that would build the biggest safehouse restoration facility in all of Central America.

Michele and I felt like God was in this project. He had aligned the pieces perfectly. The friendships, the experiences, the God-opportunities, there was no fathomable way that we could have ever made any of this happen. Once in the United States, we raised what we could of the needed $1 million towards the project costs. Over time, the total financial costs of the project grew to be an astounding $1.8 million. While those figures could have scared any normal person, we knew that God was in control of the entire process.

This reminds me of a life principle that is important for the life of any believer when following God. It's always wise to walk slowly, take your time, and not rush into rash decisions. All throughout this process, I tried to walk in step with the Holy Spirit every day. I prayed for God to open my spiritual eyes and ears, and for Him to keep me on the straight and narrow path. I needed to be constantly aware of His inaudible voice and the nudging of His Holy Spirit.

During those first few months of fundraising, God did some tremendous miracles to remind us that we were on assignment, the correct assignment He had given us. To this day, I can still remember my first speaking engagement after arriving back in the United States. It was a September I'll never forget. We were with some friends in Pennsylvania. It was our kickoff service, and as always, we experienced the jitters. It never mattered how often we spoke in public settings; the jitters always accompanied us. But when one tries to communicate God's word in the way He wants it presented, jitters are always healthy. They keep you dependent on God. That service was definitely one of those in which we wanted to be God-dependent.

The crowd was immense. Michele and I tag-teamed during the presentation, and our good friend Phil Baker, one of our biggest cheerleaders, accompanied us. God is tremendous in that He always knows how to put exceptional people into your life. Phil Baker, for us, is one of those people. Phil has since transitioned from his role as a missions coordinator to a founding role for an online ministry studies program.[26] Still, he'll continue to be a special person in our lives and hearts.

When we finished sharing our vision for Costa Rica and our hopes to build an amazing ninety-person shelter for victims of human trafficking in Costa Rica, Phil supported us wholeheartedly. The church he served and our great friends were also committed. He gave the people thirty days to respond to the offering opportunity for the project. God's people generously responded by giving an offering that was more than we ever imagined possible. I had never seen an offering of that size. A response like that seemed like God was yelling at us through a bullhorn, "You're on the right path." What a great blessing!

God speaks in different ways to different people, but His message was coming through loud and clear for us. We knew for sure God was in this. Michele said to me one day, "Aren't you afraid something bad is about to happen? Things seem like they are going way too well."

Life is definitely a rollercoaster of events—of that, you can be sure. If you're waiting for the shoe to drop because things are going too well, my advice is to stay in the present. It's easy to get ahead of ourselves, to get outside of ourselves, but when you stay in the present, you eliminate the worry and the questioning. Is staying in the present biblical? When Jesus taught His disciples how to pray, He said, "Our Father which art in heaven, give us today our daily bread" (Matthew 6:9-11). That seems to be a clear example of seeking God for our daily needs. He is responsible for tomorrow, for next year, for the things beyond our control. Stay in the present. Staying in the present doesn't eliminate our humanness to want to control life, but it does help us to learn to depend upon God. I love how the author Vaneetha Rendall Risner described this daily bread principle:

After my lament, I was quiet. I had said all I wanted to say. And then I waited. I'm not sure if I was expecting a response from God, but I knew I needed to be still and listen. In the silence, the following words came to my mind: "I'm not asking you to live like this for the rest of your life. I'm asking you to live like this today." It felt like God was speaking to me. Immediately, an unmistakable sense of peace settled over me. My situation was unchanged, but I felt strangely different. Today was a finite period that I could focus on. Today seemed doable. Today was much less frightening than "the rest of my life." Coping with anything today seemed possible. Possible, that is, with God.[27]

For the next few months, the miracles continued to surprise us. We had a God-vision with incredible potential, and unless God came through, we had no way of ever following through. Unless we had His helping hand, we wouldn't have accomplished this remarkable ministry center for so many amazing ladies. But it was as if God had given us an unanticipated gift. We were able to stand on the shoulders of someone else who had done some extraordinary work well before we became missionaries. At that point, we were officially engaged in a project that would affect the lives of so many, and God was so gracious. Whereas my plan was initially to go to Cuba, we had some very unexpected detours on our way. Instead, we were led to a place where it seemed like ministry, even God's divine will for our lives, was unfolding miraculously right before our eyes.

Allow God to Orchestrate Your Life

That Sunday when we were with Phil and our friends in Pennsylvania, it turned out to be our first miracle service. Michele and I shared about the life of Joseph. If I could only talk about two people in the Bible outside of Jesus, it would definitely be Joseph and Peter. I feel a strong connection to these two men. The Bible is full of wisdom, and God used stories to transfer that wisdom to us. But more important than the stories are the people He used. He wanted us to know He uses people like you and me. If you dig into the Scriptures, you'll discover that there's someone with whom you identify. That's the point. The Bible is not some out-of-this world book that has no application to you and me. The Bible is forever relevant! The Bible is God's story for people in the first century and the twenty-first century and beyond.

Joseph never sought God to be the most spectacular human being in the world. He took care of sheep for a living. He was young, naïve, and inexperienced. Yet, God still reached down from heaven to a boy who was willing to be sensitive to His gentle proddings. God gave him dreams that would change the world and used him to create the family lineage of Jesus Christ. Through the study of the Scriptures, commentaries, and other writers, I was surprised to learn that, time and again, those who looked at Joseph failed to see what God saw. If you were to focus on Joseph's brothers (Genesis 37), the Midianites who purchased him (Genesis 37:28-36), or even Potiphar's wife (Genesis 39:1-20), you'd discover that in each of these accounts, Joseph's life didn't seem to matter. This man later endured two years of undeserved, brutal imprisonment (Genesis 41:1). Stanley Horton said, "This was another test for Joseph, the test of delay, a difficult test for anyone. But God's delays are not cruel... God's timing is always right."[28]

Do others fail to see your potential —what God sees in you? Do you feel as though God has led you into seasons of delay? We all know what it's like to be judged, counted out, or abandoned.

I worked with one young Costa Rican boy who we'll call Arnell. Our organization was giving some of his family members help because of reasons of sexual abuse. Other boys in the neighborhood had been sexually abusing Arnell. Without divulging all the details, these boys had forced fifteen-year-old Arnell to perform sex acts. According to international law, this is a severe form of human trafficking. Because of what he experienced, he decided to become a homosexual. When I started working with Arnell, the other kids chastised him because of his choices. But Arnell wasn't alone. All around the Clinica Biblica area of downtown San Jose, there's a large presence of male cross-dressers. I never imagined myself working with this population, but God had other plans. Tammy, a psychologist at our partner organization, had begun to work with these men. Early on, she realized that it would be more beneficial to have a Spirit-led man involved in the restoration and discipling process. God led me to become that man.

Arnell wasn't the first person I counseled who had experienced severe sexual abuse. The day Tammy came to me and asked, "Roberto, will you help me with my group?" I didn't know what to say. What could I say? There was a need, God was able, and I had to be willing to say yes. So, I said, "Yes."

When her group of five men and I started working together, I wasn't sure what to expect. As I never had a conversation with anyone claiming to be a cross-dresser up until that point, it was brand-new territory for me. We had to work slowly. We asked all of the men to tell their stories, and their stories moved me. I can't stereotype or generalize, but compassion welled up in me as these men opened up. They softened my heart to a degree I had never experienced before. One guy I'll call Richy shared the first time the police arrested him. At the time when he was arrested, the penal system was totally different from what it is now. The police lined up every alleged cross-dresser and made them stand nude in a police lineup. The police then mocked and ridiculed these men as they hosed them until they were soaking wet.

"What led you into this lifestyle?" I asked.

Richy's reply was painful, yet honest. He said, "When I was a kid, I was forced to stay in the hospital for a period of time. The priest's office was at the end of the hall on my floor. My memories of that room continue to haunt me. When I was taken behind closed doors, I was forced to do things, sexual things that no kid should experience."

His words broke me. I was speechless.

Other men said, "I like to wear women's lingerie. It makes me feel comfortable." One time one of the guys called me "my love." They shared stories of oil injections into their pectorals and other practices to hide their male identities.

These horrifying stories changed me. I made a commitment to these men to walk them through a process of healing and change. I was willing to help them discover what it meant to have a relationship with Jesus Christ. Some people ridiculed me for being willing to connect with these men on this level. One lady said, "Yeah, Roberto doesn't know what he is doing. He's been taking men out for lunch. These men are saying that they have a thing going on." She wanted to discourage and belittle me, but all she did was play into my story of making me even more determined to fight for the underdog. I was confident in who I was and what God called me to do.

I identified with Joseph, and maybe you do too. It's those closest to you, often your trusted religious friends, who easily discard you. Maybe you, too, have had a Joseph experience like these sexually exploited men and women. Have you been in situations where people discarded your thoughts, your words, and ideas, you as a person? Where people made you feel worthless?

Genesis 37 relates that a seventeen-year-old boy was so hated by his brothers that they threw him into a pit only to sell him as a slave. Joseph begged and pleaded for his life (Genesis 42:21), but sadly, it made no difference. Skip over to Genesis 39:2-3. Amazingly, instead of becoming bitter, Joseph trusted God and did everything as unto the Lord. As a slave, he served his master in such a way that pleased and honored God. Joseph had such confidence in God's promises that he was willing to commit whatever he did and whatever happened to him to the Lord.

He spent thirteen years going through a whirlwind of mishaps and blessings until one day he had the ultimate opportunity to punish his brothers (Genesis 50:19-20). Somehow, he recognized that amidst everything, he wasn't God. He had to leave room for God to deal with the past. There's no way this was even the slightest bit easy. When he had the opportunity to exact revenge, he realized that although his experiences were hard, God had never lost sight of his purpose. Through his brothers' anger and injustice toward him, Joseph realized that was God's way to use him to save many peoples' lives. Joseph was positioned to hear from God. Joseph was sensitive. Joseph is an example of exactly why the Bible is so relevant.

Joseph's life story is symbolic of how Jesus paid the price so that you and I could inherit eternity. It's a story of how two young people and their kids from New Jersey would one day be detoured to Costa Rica. It's a story of how God would make a way for us to minister to girls that had been thrown into the trafficking pit of despair. It's a story of how these same girls would have the opportunity to trust in the God who creates beauty out of ashes, joy out of mourning, and praise out of despair (Isaiah 61:3). Because Joseph allowed God to orchestrate his life, his life had a purpose. His purpose reached through time to let us know what is possible when we're sensitive enough to hear from God himself.

IT ALL FALLS APART

You might hear the news from a policeman: "I'm sorry.
He didn't survive the accident." You might return a
friend's call, only to be told, "The surgeon brought
bad news." Too many spouses have heard these words
from grim-faced soldiers: "We regret to inform you..."
In such moments, spring becomes winter, blue turns
to gray, birds go silent, and the chill of sorrow settles
in. It's cold in the valley of the shadow of death.[29]

What a grim way to start the chapter. All of a sudden, we encountered an unexpected turn for the worst. "Unexpected." That was the theme of our story for 2018. Michele and I had experienced incredible confirmations from God that Costa Rica was our assignment, when all of a sudden, the floor fell out from under us! Michele's fears that something bad was going to happen were finally realized.

While we had been fundraising in the United States, things were going better than well. God was doing miracles left and right. We maintained communication with our partner organization in Costa Rica when *pink flags* began to appear. *Pink flags* is an idiom I use to describe events, conversations, or observations that are difficult to categorize as *red flags*. Normally, when using the *red flag* descriptor in conversations, the speaker is indicating the warning of a bad or dangerous situation. On the other hand, the *pink flag* means that there is the potential for there to be a *red*

flag. It is in these *pink flag* moments when I have to tell myself, "Bob, be cautious, be alert. Something seems off, but you could be wrong." *Pink flags* do not always turn red, but living with caution as a life principle when making decisions or living life is always a good practice.

Looking back on my fundraising journey, I realize some warnings (*pink flags*) were easy to recognize, but I wasn't able to identify them. We had been intimately involved with our ministry partner organization in Costa Rica for four years; there were no large sums of money involved in the relationship. We financed certain events, helped as needed, and did what we could. After we arrived in the United States, our Costa Rican partner organization was wiped out by a robbery. Raquel called us and broke down in tears. In one day, criminals had destroyed the organization she had spent her life building—and not just any criminals. It had been a premeditated crime involving the on-duty guard. The thieves stole every computer, the kitchen and sewing supplies, the second-floor safe, and everything of value.

Our friend was devastated, but we did what we could to help. Our first response was to send out a Facebook post seeking financial help during this great crisis. Our United States friends responded generously, and we were able to send close to $16,000 to get everything back up and running. While the money raised didn't cover all of the expenses, it was enough to get the organization back on its feet, providing services to our ladies and their families.

The first *pink flag* that made its debut after we sent the much needed money was the flag of gratitude. Weeks later, the communication trail went silent. There were no thank-yous, no letters of gratitude. From the few conversations we had, it seemed as if the monetary gifts were perceived by our partner organization as unwritten expectations rather than acts of generosity. Tensions later ensued over what I would consider standard practices that should have been a given in partner organizations.

To try a strengthen the bond between our partner organization and us, Michele and I agreed to invite Raquel to accompany us for a few speaking engagements in the United States. With many churches hosting overseas missions awareness conventions at that particular time, we managed to have her join us. That was when the second *pink flag* went up sky high!

We attended a morning missions convention followed by a mission banquet in the evening at our home church of Calvary Assemblies of God in Pennsauken. The church rented a hall, set up an amazing program, and, thanks be to God, invited us to be keynote speakers with a twenty-minute speaking cap. Raquel joined us, and I wanted her to greet the people. During the earlier morning meeting, I asked her to give a short greeting, and she disregarded what I had asked her to do. Her greeting, way beyond the boundaries of a greeting, made it very difficult to share within the church's time allotment. That concerned me, but I didn't say anything. It made me wonder what she was going to do or say at the banquet that evening.

The banquet venue had a time limitation, so the guest speaker needed to keep the message to twenty minutes per the church's request. I introduced Raquel, asking her to greet the crowd, and then handed her the microphone. Trusting she'd only give a short greeting, she spoke for twenty-five minutes! Instead of a greeting, she preached an entire sermon full of chastisement. I was confused about how to respond. I didn't want to humiliate her or take the microphone away—but she had used up my time. She exceeded the time limit, and neither Michele nor myself managed to say a word. I apologized to the pastor afterward and was thankful he understood. But those two speaking moments should have been screaming *pink flags* for my attention.

I wanted God to give direction in those two services. I thought, "God, I'm sweating here; please tell me what to do." But He didn't. I had to grapple with those emotions while also trying to be led by the Spirit. Life has repeatedly taught me that there's a strong correlation between being effectively led by the Spirit and having enough of God's word in your mind and heart. As Christ's followers, it's our responsibility to get God's word inside of us. No one can do it for us. Jesus warned, "Watch out for false prophets. They come to you in sheep's clothing, but inwardly they are ferocious wolves" (Matthew 7:15). The so-called prophets to which Jesus referred were the religious teachers of that era. The Jamieson-Fausset-Brown Bible Commentary speaks of these people as those who come "as authorized expounders of the mind of God and guides to heaven."[30] In other words, they look religious and might even sound religious. That's scary. Jesus speaks to you and me in 2021, "Be on the lookout, but more importantly, be prepared!"

Think about when Paul said to Timothy, "Until I get there, focus on reading the Scriptures to the church, encouraging the believers, and teaching them... Keep a close watch on how you live and on your teaching. Stay true to what is right for the sake of your own salvation and the salvation of those who hear you" (1 Timothy 4:13, 16). Paul dedicated a large portion of his letters to correcting false teaching and protecting believers while guiding them in their faith. We're no more exempt than they were from false teaching, and we should be alert, watchful, and prepared.

Raquel never violated anything in the Scriptures. She never said anything that didn't line up with the Bible, yet something felt off. As she was speaking, my antennae were up because I sensed something wasn't right for the second time, but I didn't know what it was. Other than the abuse of time, nothing was wrong. I didn't address the issue after the service. I tried to overlook the discrepancy and keep my eyes on the prize, the future. Maybe I should have confronted her, but I believe I did the right thing by not overreacting.

Timing is always critical. Part of discerning timing is hearing from God. God will most likely never speak audibly in those moments, but that doesn't mean He is silent. We have to pay attention to that internal voice of the Spirit that tugs on our hearts and spirits. The Holy Spirit is a gentleman in every sense of the word. He is never going to force His will on you or anyone.

Deuteronomy of the Old Testament records that the people were given the following instruction,

> Today I am giving you a choice. You can choose life and success or death and disaster. I am commanding you to be loyal to the Lord, to live the way he has told you, and to obey his laws and teachings. You are about to cross the Jordan River and take the land that he is giving you. If you obey him, you will live and become successful and powerful (Deuteronomy 30:15-16 CEV).

God has not changed. He gives you and me those same "if" choices. Thank God I was paying attention that day because my response would impact the way we related to Raquel in the future. Those services opened my eyes, not to overt problems, but *pink flags* that could quickly become *red flags.*

When we finally returned to Costa Rica, fully funded, our relationship with Raquel had definitively changed. I was now responsible for a large sum of money that we needed to channel to the construction of the shelter. If anything went wrong or money was mishandled, people weren't going to take it up with her; they'd single me out. It was a great responsibility. Thinking of all the lives that were going to be impacted by this place, I knew everything had to be honest and legal at all times with total transparency.

The weight of that responsibility fell heavily upon me. I thought of the sacrifice our friends in Pennsylvania made that first incredible Sunday morning of fundraising. I wanted them to be proud and know that every penny would go into making the shelter project a success. To be honest, my relationship with Raquel needed to change.

The ensuing months presented us with many growth opportunities. We grew incredibly close with the board of directors. We had great people, a great staff, and we were impacting lives for eternity. Michele developed material on discipleship that would fill a four-inch binder. She worked tirelessly because she knew the impact she was having. She knew that God put a story in her that had to be told. It was a story of redemption, a story of hope. We both knew that we were not just making an earthly difference. The stakes of ministry were high, and we knew that eternity would be different for so many of our beneficiaries because we were choosing to trust God.

One of the blessings about the way our partner organization was set up was that there was an all-population church service at least once a month. Michele led the ladies weekly in small group discipleship, and I led the staff in their small group pod. Everyone knew that a Christ-centered faith was central to everything we did. However, that didn't eliminate our humanity. We still had to work together as people, and like the disciples, we all needed to be reminded "to love one another." Some growth opportunities resulted from normal, healthy organizational operations, while other situations would have made life a whole lot easier if they never happened.

The last board meeting at our partner organization was, without a doubt, one of those growth opportunities that I'd rather have avoided. Tensions had been mounting over several issues, and the board had been struggling to get a handle on some out-of-control administrative issues. Then, everything exploded as the floor fell out from under us. God himself designed a painful lesson to teach us that sometimes there are delays ahead, and we need to be prepared to stop.

When we arrived at the board meeting, there were more attendees than just the board members. Two lawyers were present that no one knew except for Raquel. As the meeting began, we discovered the minutes book had been confiscated. Unsure who took it, the board of directors felt its disappearance was an intentional act to freeze any future decision-making. Raquel explained why her lawyers were present. She was taking back control of the organization, eliminating all of the board members except for Michele and me. She wanted to keep us on board because we had been funding the construction of the shelter. And that was part of the tension.

When we had signed onto the project, the handshake agreement was that we'd have a fifty-fifty partnership. Sadly, our partner organization wasn't fulfilling its obligations in raising the other half of the money. In addition, any money they raised in Costa Rica for the shelter was used on operational expenses at our main site. That day we were reduced to nothing more than a bankrolling institution. When I pushed back at the meeting, Raquel said, "I'm God's anointed one." Her words blew me away.

By the time all was said and done, the board was effectively dismissed. The bank became concerned over what was taking place and froze all of the accounts that December. The staff had to go through the holidays without any pay or the guarantee of a job at the end of that month. The minutes book was gone, Raquel decided to leave the country until after the holidays, lawyers were involved, and lawsuits were filed that would ultimately involve the Costa Rican Department of Labor. The situation was horrible.

We moved to the second floor with the board to discuss our next steps. We all knew there was a battle raging. As we sat and discussed the next best plan of action, I realized that I was sidelined without the board. They were my friends, my protection. Without them by my side, I couldn't continue in a healthy way with our partner organization. I also knew God had set me on this path and had lined up the pieces along the way. The ministry there in Costa Rica was perfect, so how could this be happening? If God were in it, how could everything fall apart right before our eyes? Our friends in the United States had enabled us to build this wonderful shelter for so many incredibly amazing ladies. I felt the weight of my responsibility again, and it was heavy.

As our board gathered at the table that day to discuss the events, I had to make an unexpected decision. With our partner organization in extreme disarray and my board colleagues uprooted from their positions, our continued partnership with this organization was over. It would obviously be best if we dissolved it. I never dreamed this could happen. I struggled with this drastic solution. Michele was just as perplexed. We talked about walking away from the project with heavy hearts. We had already invested all of the raised funds in the construction, many groups had come and gone, and since the beginning of the construction, we were all in. When we proposed to our board colleagues that it be best if we dissolved the partnership, each one understood completely. It was unbelievably hard that day, but the goal was never a political power play to wield some level of authority. This project was about building God's kingdom. It was about creating a place where ladies wouldn't only discover restoration but also what it meant to have a relationship with Jesus Christ.

No one in the Bible ever said that it would be easy to follow Jesus. In fact, when Jesus sent out His disciples, He told them:

> If anyone will not welcome you or listen to your words, leave that home or town and shake the dust off your feet... I am sending you out like sheep among wolves. Therefore be as shrewd as snakes and as innocent as doves. Be on your guard; you will be handed over to the local councils and be flogged in the synagogues. On my account you will be brought before governors and kings as witnesses to them and to the Gentiles. But when they arrest you, do not worry about what to say or how to say it. At that time you will be given what to say, for it will not be you speaking, but the Spirit of your Father speaking through you.

> Brother will betray brother to death, and a father his child; children will rebel against their parents and have them put to death. You will be hated by everyone because of me, but the one who stands firm to the end will be saved. When you are persecuted in one place, flee to another. Truly I tell you, you will not finish

going through the towns of Israel before the Son of Man comes (Matthew 10:14, 16-23).

From the beginning, Jesus made sure His disciples knew what to expect. The challenge of what lay ahead brought these men to the end of themselves. They all wrestled with what it meant to be a follower of Jesus Christ. Jesus knows the power of human emotions. He understands emotions are powerful and play a big role in our lives. Jesus's words needed to resonate with His disciples so that they remembered the assignment He gave them when things got tough. They needed to look beyond the impulse of emotions. They had to rely on His words.

There's no doubt that God allowed us to have His written Word to help us do the same. I wholeheartedly believe that Jesus knew that we, like the disciples, would have to learn to look beyond our emotions and trust God even when He doesn't make sense. The guidance and wisdom we need are in His written Word. "Your word is a lamp to guide my feet and a light for my path" (Psalm 119:105).

For my particular situation, we were being delayed, and we had to be prepared to stop. In hindsight, I now understand why. However, during that crisis, God was stopping me. He was speaking to me, maybe even yelling at me in a very unorthodox way, but I didn't hear His voice right away. In all honesty, our successes and achievements up to that point had distracted us from hearing God.

The ongoing tensions had reached a boiling point which signaled the end of a tremendous season in our lives. Sadly, as Peter Scazzero said:

> Our society doesn't teach endings. Our churches don't teach endings. Our families don't equip us to embrace endings as part of the rhythm of life. When we add

our own insecurities and fears, it seems obvious that
we consider endings as interruptions to be avoided no
matter what it takes. The problem is that, in the process, we block the new beginnings God wants to birth
in and through us.[31]

We weren't prepared for the end. We never anticipated this
ending, and it was challenging, trying to hear God's voice amidst
all of the noise. While Raquel was out of the country, I continued
for weeks to give morning devotionals for the staff. All the
while, I firmly believed God would soon intervene and correct
the wrongness of the situation. He never did. To make mat-
ters worse, the chaos of that day eventually found its way into
our marriage and affected our mental health. While my faith in
God continued to be strong, there was no avoiding the fact that
somehow God went almost dead silent for nearly the next eighteen months of our lives. It was an experience I pray never repeats
itself in my life or my story.

Inside suffering is the seed of change[32]

GOD GOES FULL-ON RADIO-SILENT

...even when we can't discern that anything redemptive could emerge from our loss. The key is to be willing to wait. And while we wait, we spend extended amounts of time alone with God. We process our thoughts and emotions with others or in a journal. We position ourselves as expectant pilgrims on a journey we listen and learn, looking for and expecting to see signs of new life.[33]

As I struggled with what was happening, my wife battled her own war. Below, Michele tells her story in her own words:

On February 2 at 2:00 AM, I felt my heart beating in my chest as never before. For the next four hours, I was constantly awakened from deep sleep to my heart pounding and found myself dripping with sweat. I didn't understand what was going on as I cried out to the Lord, "Father, please help me!" At 6:00 AM, I couldn't take it anymore and made my way downstairs, threw myself on the floor, and begged the Lord to make it stop.

At 8:33 AM, I sent a text in despair to fellow missionary wives in Costa Rica. I call them my prayer warriors. That November, we had a powerful retreat where our area director spoke about the different seasons of our lives. I had realized back then that I was in the winter. After the retreat, we had started a group chat where we shared our prayer requests. I asked if they could come over that morning and pray with me.

They graciously came, and as we talked, they reminded me of all that we had been through those last few months. The ministry we had poured our hearts and souls into for seven years was over! We had fought so hard to try to make things work. We had invested seven incredible years and were in the middle of a huge building project. We never expected that we'd have to walk away from that ministry. I could never get closure and say a proper goodbye to the women and teens I had grown to love so much. I was grieving my loss, and my body was reacting to the grief my heart felt. On top of that, we were still adjusting to dropping our oldest daughter off at college, and doctors had recently diagnosed my husband with an autoimmune disease. We felt as though our lives and ministry were under complete attack.

My doctor recommended I start taking an antidepressant immediately. I've never been a huge medication person and knew nothing about antidepressants, which made me very scared. My mind couldn't get past the stigma surrounding the idea of being on this medication. I prayed and pleaded for the Lord to relieve my body of these symptoms.

I fought against taking the medication for about three weeks until my doctor said, "Michele, you have been through a lot this past year, and your mind and body need help." I knew very little about anxiety and depression at that point. My journey with mental illness was only beginning. I wish I could say that the medication worked overnight. It was a battle for me to trust the process. Another fellow missionary was there to encourage me and shared with me how the medication worked for her.

Owing to some side effects the first three months, I decided to stop taking the medication. I felt fine for about a month and a half, and then the depression and anxiety returned with a vengeance. I didn't understand; I was praying and seeking the Lord, and all of our friends and family were praying for me. The anxiety became so bad that I was afraid of being alone. Paranoid and terrified of the dark, it felt as though the walls were closing in on me. I lost twelve pounds. Many of our friends started asking what was going on, but I was embarrassed to admit I was having problems.

It made me feel like a weak Christian. My husband struggled to keep things running in our home while being worried and frustrated about not knowing what to do. This situation was the biggest spiritual attack we'd ever faced, and we were all growing tired.

Over the next ten months, God had to work in miraculous ways to restore the Michele everyone knew. On October 19, 2018, she woke up to write the following journal entry:

Lord, today you have restored to me the joy of my salvation. You brought me here to heal my heart. God, I now see that you wanted me all to yourself. I feel free today, free to dance, free to laugh. Yes, laugh, something the enemy tried to rob from me. It has been a long road, but you have never left my side. You were here all along. You even sent friends to visit me. My mind is at peace, just as Isaiah 26:3 says, "You will keep in perfect peace all whose minds are stayed on you because they trust in you."

It was a long and scary journey, and I never want to return to that place. But it was the prayers of many people that pulled me through. You will never know just how much missionaries covet your prayers. Whether you're living abroad or serving in the United States, we all desperately need prayer. The enemy is constantly at our heels with discouragement, fear, anxiety, depression, and more. He would love nothing more than to see us all fail. In the ministry where we were involved, spiritual warfare was huge. We were ripping lives from the claws of Satan. Looking back, it doesn't surprise me that the enemy tried to take our family out. However, thanks to the many prayer warriors that have stood with us, we will continue in the fight.

Radio Silence

It seemed as if God went full-on radio-silent December 2017. The next time I heard the Lord speak was for a moment in October 2018 and then again in June 2019, some eighteen months later—only twice in those grueling months. However, when God spoke, I was able to hear, I understood, yes! God's timing is perfect. For Michele to experience her God-moment, she had to discover God's timing on her own and in her own way. She spent thirty days in Florida in October 2018, while Isabella and I stayed in Costa Rica. Michele went away to be with God, and God met with her in a special way. I'm so grateful she found Him.

My journey was somewhat different. I had already accepted that God delayed us. While I wasn't prepared to stop, we had no other choice. Our ministry landscape was changing without my approval or having any idea what God was doing. That's what makes Him God. He doesn't need our approval. He needs our obedience.

When God called Abraham to leave his home, his land, his people, He also gave Abraham the miracle of a son. This man was old, and he had no business having a son, but here we go again; what business do we have telling God what He needs to do? In Genesis 22:2, God told Abraham, "Take your son, your only son

173

Isaac, whom you love, and go to the land of Moriah, and offer him there as a burnt offering on one of the mountains of which I shall tell you." What did God say? God had given Abraham a miracle child in his old age, yet He asked Abraham to sacrifice that same son when He called him to follow. Would you follow this God? Could you obey?

Thank God, I've never been in that position. I don't know if I would have been capable of doing what Abraham did. Following God will always entail steps of obedience that will stretch us in our walk of faith. The harsh reality is that all too often, those around you will never understand the gravity of the decisions you make when following Jesus. I have wrestled with many of the decisions we've made in ministry. The prayers of our friends back in the United States are so crucial. Please let me encourage you to pray not only for us as missionaries but also for your pastors.

I will never forget the words of 1 Peter 5:8, which says, "Stay alert! Watch out for your great enemy, the devil. He prowls around like a roaring lion, looking for someone to devour." While the devil isn't flesh and blood like you and me, I can assure you that he is still very real. There is a battle that rages in the heavenlies. Satan would love to destroy God's church. He would love to destroy any chance you and I have of experiencing a relationship with Jesus Christ. I'm truly grateful for the men and women who have accepted the challenge to take faith steps daily in the ministry like Abraham. There are ministers worldwide who have made life choices to ensure that people like you and me can hear this good news of the Gospel. Engaging in missions and engaging in pastoral ministry goes beyond us as individuals. It's all about Jesus's mission to seek and save the lost, no matter the cost.

I'm sure your pastor will never publicly share his challenges in shepherding God's people. I'm quite confident you will never hear a missionary discussing the ups and downs of cross-cultural living. For those of us in ministry, we just accept it and move on. We realize that what we do has eternal significance.

Abraham, too, realized that God called him. He could take his son to that mountaintop, because despite the pain God's request caused him, he knew he could trust God!

Please, let me encourage you to pray for your missionaries, your pastors, your spiritual leaders. Some say being a pastor is like living in a fishbowl. When you're a pastor, everyone sees you; they see your family and your ups and downs. Sadly, when you're not perfect, you may even become the weekly topic of conversation, whether in person or behind your back. For those that have chosen to follow God into the ministry, I applaud you. Maybe you find yourself in a position where there's no other choice but to rely on Him. Don't give up! Yes, God does give strength, He gives hope. The struggles of life never disappear, but God can be trusted.

I naively got into missions, not knowing the traps, struggles, or challenges that awaited me. Guaranteed: most pastors are exactly the same. When speaking of pastors that went through the worldwide COVID pandemic, George Barna told us:

> Three in 10 pastors (31%) say they are currently strug-
> gling the most with their emotional well-being, while
> a quarter (26%) says this about their relational well-
> being... Taking a longer view of some of the emotions
> brought on by the pandemic, a majority of pastors
> (68%) say they have felt overwhelmed regularly in the
> last four weeks (21% frequently, 47% sometimes), a
> testament to the effect the crisis is having on church
> leaders' decisions.[34]

The Assemblies of God wrote:

> Pastors often enter ministry with a mental picture of
> lush, gentle hills surrounded by placid sheep grazing
> on pastures as a caring shepherd watches over them.
> Pastors also picture the smaller church as a tran-
> quil place where people gather while a well-equipped
> and loving shepherd feeds them spiritually... At times,

however, docile sheep can turn into malicious beasts, viciously snapping with sharpened fangs at the heels of a fleeing shepherd. As a result, pastors leave the ministry feeling hurt, abandoned, and abused. They may question their call to ministry, the meaning of Christian fellowship, and even doubt the love and compassion of God.[35]

I have to admit; these statistics scare me. Now think about Abraham. He had no statistics of overcomers, no statistics on current trends of those serving God; all he had was an encounter where God called him. God appeared to seventy-five-year-old Abraham and said,

Go from your country, your people and your father's household to the land I will show you. I will make you into a great nation, and I will bless you; I will make your name great, and you will be a blessing. I will bless those who bless you, and whoever curses you I will curse; and all peoples on earth will be blessed through you (Genesis 12:1-3).

There was no conversation about a miracle baby, much less a conversation about the day when God would tell Abraham to sacrifice his only child. God left Abraham in the dark.

Why?

God knows we don't need all of the details. The details would scare us. If God had told me what missions would cost me, I might not have become a missionary at all, and then I'd have had no miracles to share or experiences to tell. God kept me in the dark. What did he ask of Abraham? The same thing He asks of me and you—Obedience. God is not in the business of letting everyone called into ministry know how their future will play out because they'd then try to control it. That's our human nature. We want to control. But God needs to be in control. God knows the bigger picture, and He knows what you and I need to know. Jesus's famous words were "Follow me." He didn't say where nor how. Simply, "Follow me." We all have to decide every day if we will follow or control. Scazzero reminded us:

> Change is difficult for most people. We experience it as an unwelcome intruder derailing our hopes and plans. We prefer to remain in control and to operate in familiar patterns, even when they fail to serve us well. We might acknowledge intellectually that God can bring new beginnings and precious gifts out of our losses, but it somehow doesn't ease the sting of loss or prevent us from trying to avoid it. It isn't easy to trust the inner voice of the Spirit inviting us to cross over into this painful and unknown new territory.[36]

Abraham could have tried to control the situation. So can you and I, but it's at the intersection of human will and obedience that God is allowed to be God. Abraham trusted, climbed the mountain, and raised the knife when suddenly "the angel of the Lord called out to him from heaven, "Abraham! Abraham!" "Here I am," he replied. "Do not lay a hand on the boy," he said. "Do not do anything to him. Now I know that you fear God, because you have not withheld from me your son, your only son" (Genesis 22:11-12). While God would never force Abraham to be obedient, He required obedience. The blessing required obedience. It still does.

While Michele was away for those thirty days in Florida, I visited my general doctor, a licensed psychologist, and a psychiatrist. Michele was away trying to hear from God, but I, too, was at home trying to figure out how to cope. God was silent, and all I had were questions. I told my doctor, "Doc, I'm not right. This whole situation has obliterated me, and I need help. If that means an antidepressant, I'm ready." He gave me a prescription that day. All I can say is thank God that He never told me my future when I was a naïve kid, wrestling with thoughts of being a missionary—especially when many of my life experiences indicated it would never happen. I was at my lowest.

In my first visit with the psychiatrist, I felt uneasy. He wanted me to describe my feelings in a tangible way that he could understand. I had to go beyond the use of just descriptive words. My doctor wanted me to create an abstract picture that would let him see how I saw myself, regarding my feelings.

"Tell me, what's going on?" he asked me.

I was clueless on how to respond. Still, I tried to put my feelings into a picture story I could easily tell. "Well, it's almost like I fell into a gigantic pit with no way out. I'm at the bottom and see how tall the walls are. It's obvious I can't get out. No matter what I do, I'll slip right back down. I'm sitting at the bottom of this pit, right in the middle. I can see the sky, the clouds, the sun. And I know I'm not getting out. I sit there and stare. That's all I can do."

We talked for about forty-five minutes, and I left with some medicine and a follow-up appointment. Oh, joy.

My outlook on life wasn't the best; however, God was prepping the ground to get a crucial message into my heart. One Wednesday evening, I sat down to watch *SEAL Team*, one of my favorite shows, but the TV wouldn't stream the program. I felt frustrated. Isabella had argued with me earlier, complaining about my cooking. She had said my pork chops tasted like leather, and I was determined she would eat what I cooked. The night didn't go as planned.

I had a Thursday afternoon appointment scheduled with my psychologist. Isabella had left for school, and I had the wonderful opportunity to speak about my feelings again to my psychologist on my computer screen. However, that day we talked about Michele. The psychologist said, "I haven't been able to speak with Michele. How has she been doing?" I gave her an update, and we talked about leaving Costa Rica early to return to the United States. I said I wasn't going back unless Michele thought it was necessary. The psychologist replied, "Bob, I don't know if you can put that decision on her after all she's been through." I wasn't convinced, but we had a good call and hung up.

That night in June 2019, God spoke for the first time since that October 2018 board room meeting. I managed to find the *SEAL Team* show again on TV, so I sat down for some "me time" while Isabella was out with her friends. The main actor, a Bravo One in charge of an elite SEAL team, had been going through some family turmoil following the death of his wife. Whenever his pager rang, he was responsible for responding, a practice that required immediate deployment at any time. His kids were grieving the death of their mother, and in the midst of all this, he did what most guys do best, he pushed forward. In Spanish, there is a saying, "Put your pants on and grab your machete." He had his machete, and his kids hated him for it. His daughter was at all-out war with her dad. "Dad, Mom died! You don't just move on. You have to take time to grieve."

A few minutes later, Bravo One stood in his superior's office, making a case for himself to step away from the team. During his discussion with his superior, Bravo One said, "Captain, I love my team. I've been with these guys through thick and thin, but my family needs me now. I need to step away from Bravo."

I wasn't sure exactly how to respond to what I heard just then. It was as if the truth was slapping me in the face. I knew I had to respond. The Holy Spirit used Bravo One to speak to me at just the right time. If I had watched the episode the day before, the message wouldn't have gotten through to me. I needed the conversation the day before with my psychologist about going home. God knew I wasn't ready that day when I couldn't watch the episode. He knew I'd talk with my counselor about going home, and he knew I needed that episode to convince me it was okay to grieve and go home. God can even speak through a show! Some might consider it an absurdity, but that's okay. God is the one who chooses how He speaks, not us! God will never be confined to a box nor a human-constructed methodology.

God's voice is extremely multifaceted, but we each need to position ourselves to learn, grow, and hear. Like riding a bike, we don't always get it the first time, but experience is a phenomenal teacher.

Right after that TV episode, I called Michele. I told her what had happened. She started crying, but I didn't know why. I didn't know if she were happy or sad. Then she said, "I was here in my room, and I knew we needed to or go back to the States, but I didn't know how to tell you." God's timing was and is perfect. Michele had her breakthrough, I had mine, and we knew things were going to get better.

The Counseling Experience

The only problem is things didn't get better. Things got worse. When we finally did decide to wrap up our term and return to the United States, a whole new set of challenges suddenly appeared. And neither of us were ready to face them. I felt like my wife was different. The days and weeks passed. Whenever I tried to address my feelings, she pushed back, responding that I was somehow wrong. We argued like cats and dogs. Almost everything led to an argument, and our arguments weren't pretty.

Christmas 2019 was one of the saddest seasons of my entire life. Our ministry had fallen apart in Costa Rica, and my wife was, at least from my point of view, a different person. We did nothing but fight, and Isabella struggled with being back in the United States. It seemed like everything about life was against us. The only reason for our return was that I had responded to what I thought was the voice of God speaking to me through an episode of *SEAL Team*. I felt discouraged and ridiculous. Then I received an email from the Assemblies of God headquarters that no one wants to receive. My Central America area director said they expected me to go for counseling since we had returned early to the States.

What was I to do? I had no choice but to submit to the process if I were to continue in missions. The situation didn't get any better with counseling. It got worse.

One weekend, I blew up on Michele, and I thought we were finished as a couple. It was a Saturday, so I reached out to my psychologist for an emergency intervention. Thank God, my psychologist responded to our plea for help. She helped talk Michele and me off the cliff while beginning to teach us about the power of time-outs. Those weeks and months were ugly. I believed our psychologist was just making things worse. I told her time and time again, "I think you're digging for stuff that's not there." She couldn't seem to get to the root issues without making her way through the weeds—what I considered to be nonessential things. Everyone builds walls; we all put up protective mechanisms, sometimes good and sometimes bad. There's nothing necessarily wrong with these behaviors; one can't deal with root issues if weeds prevent you from getting to them in the first place. Through our sessions, we eventually discovered my wife was bitter for several reasons. First, she had wanted me to go to counseling for a long time, and I had said no. This lack of desire to engage in counseling is common for men. Women tend to be talkers, whereas men express their feelings differently. I wasn't about to "counsel" with anyone until I was forced to do it. Second, she was bitter because I had been emotionally absent during her emotional journey with depression and anxiety.

Again, this is not uncommon for us guys. Many of us have to learn to connect with our feelings—something never taught on the playground. More often than not, men struggle to develop this area. In my defense, my issues were more profound than the way I was socialized as a male. I fought for and was faithful to my family, and I loved my wife with every fiber of my being. But my wife needed more than I was able to give her; I just didn't know it. She needed an emotional ear that would listen, be empathic, and walk with her in her journey without trying to fix everything. My love consisted of work and caring for my family, and while that's great, it doesn't change the fact that my wife still needed to connect with my heart.

After considerable digging, my psychologist said, "Bob, I think you need to find another psychiatrist here in the United States because your issues go beyond my help."

Great, I thought. *I'm a minister, I'm fighting with my wife, almost to the point of divorce, and I have to keep seeing a shrink.* Whether you're a minister or a truck driver, you'll never be exempt from the problems that plague us as humans. Part of following Jesus is learning to become like Jesus. Life wouldn't be life without problems that require work. And marriage requires work, humility, forgiveness, love, patience—all of the fruits of the Spirit found in Galatians, chapter 5.

Because my insurance had no nearby psychiatrists, I had to go to Delaware. Our sessions didn't start well. At the first appointment, my psychiatrist discovered that a bus had hit me twenty years before. I had been left to die, fell into a coma, and while in the hospital, my doctors diagnosed with frontal lobe brain damage. The accident explained my lack of emotion. It made total sense. My psychiatrist told me, "I can't give you a get-out-of-jail-free card, but your wife needs to understand that you're limited in your emotional capacity." I learned how to work on my emotions and better them, but because of the accident, my emotions just did not seem to flow as naturally as they might for others. I was emotionally impaired, and I didn't even know it!

How many go through life missing out on all that God has for us and never even realize it? How often does God want to speak to us, but we don't know how to hear Him? Maybe we've been in church for thirty, forty, or even fifty years, but we missed out on really getting to know a God who wants to be intimate with us. I pray that you stop right now and take a moment to talk to God. Tell Him what's going on, what you think you need, and then be quiet and listen. Sometimes we're so consumed with talking and making noise that we don't give God any space to speak. The noise is so loud because we allow it to be.

Possibly your marriage is about to crumble. As you're reading about my journey, you find yourself thinking, "Have I followed Jesus in how I connect with my husband or wife? Have I listened, really listened?" It's never too late to start. So, please do me a favor, put down this book, and do what you need to do. Talk to that person and ask for forgiveness; for once, maybe be still and listen. Quiet the noise, silence the demons, go for a walk.

I can't say that things immediately improved when we started talking about our problems in counseling. As husband and wife, it helped us understand each other, but we still had one more area of bitterness to work through. Those first three months of counseling were ugly; I mean really ugly. My psychologist even reached out to the Assemblies of God and told them, "The Pérez's aren't ready. They need more counseling, more time." Well, the amazing organization of the Assemblies of God let us know we were important. They let us know they would help us get the healing we needed, and they did. They gave us three more months to work on our problems, and we worked hard on ourselves.

I once read an amazing book by Terrence Real that changed my marriage. *The New Rules of Marriage* states, "roughly half of all marriages fail altogether."[37] This fact sounds grim, even depressing. In his book, Terrence asks some great reflective questions that allow us to understand what a great marriage really exists for those who never split apart. It continues:

> The refrain I hear over and over again from dissatisfied women is "I don't feel like I have a real partner." A partner who shares in the details of domestic life and in her concerns about the kids. An intellectual partner who cares about what she thinks and supports her development. And most of all, an emotional partner who shows interest in and appreciation for her feelings and who has a few feelings of his own to bring to the table... The shift from seeing marriage as companionship to seeing marriage as a sustained form of intimacy is a transformation of historical proportions.[38]

There's hope! Marriage can be awesome, even fulfilling, the very way God intended it to be. We must be willing to put in the work of taking steps to heal our marriage. When I started to make changes, explore my emotional self, the third reason for my wife's bitterness soon emerged. I once read that when a husband starts to do the work addressing his role in healing the relationship, his wife will resent him for doing what she hoped he'd do so long ago. In my case, Michele resented me for now participating in the counseling process because that was something she desired for a long time. Women are hard to understand. I was going for counseling, doing the work, and then she resented me for it? Yes, that's what happened exactly. Here's a fact, guys, you'll never understand women. It's a statistical improbability, but it doesn't preclude us from following Jesus and doing the work of becoming a Christ-follower in our marriage and life. As I wrote this part, Michele was sitting next to me on the plane reading this. It made her laugh in agreement.

For the next three months, I felt like God was punishing me. I had weekly appointments with my psychologist and psychiatrist. Each one assigned me homework tasks. The homework was really the punishment. Because of my psychiatric diagnosis, my counselor had said, "Alright, we have a diagnosis, so now we to have rediscover your emotions." She then gave me writing assignments. First, my psychologist expected me to put into written words my thoughts about my marriage. Secondly, I had to describe my feelings connected to those thoughts. And lastly, she added a journaling exercise during which I had to write about what I was feeling at different moments of the day. With this exercise, I was also expected to describe where I felt those feelings in my body.

What kind of bologna is this? I wondered. *Not only do I have to describe my feelings, but I have to talk about where I feel it in my body? How ridiculous.* Sometimes ridiculousness works. Why do you think God chose *SEAL Team* to minister to me? We all have quirks and idiosyncrasies. The neat thing about God is that He uses those quirks to get our attention. Over the next three months, God worked a miracle. We managed to get back to a place of healing and wholeness. It wasn't all smooth sailing. It was hard work, work which hasn't ended yet. None of us will completely be like Jesus this side of eternity. That's intentional. God demands obedience so that we can rely on him daily for everything, and I mean everything, that we need.

This isn't the end of the story—there's more. *Is God finished with His miracles?* I asked myself many times. Since that day in the boardroom, God had only spoken once, and I still don't know why any of this happened. He continued to be silent.

One day Michele and I were having dinner at the Olive Garden in Springfield near the Assemblies of God headquarters. My heart was heavy because it was time to begin fundraising to go back to the mission field. I didn't know if I was ready. I wasn't even sure we could go back to Costa Rica after all of the trauma we had experienced. While I've tried to capture much of what took place in Costa Rica, time doesn't allow me to go into every detail of the betrayal, hurt, and discouragement we felt. I sometimes wish God would let me forget some of those details. The pain of my memory often makes it hard to move on, even hard to forgive. So that night at dinner, I told Michele, "Hon, I think we either go back to the mission field and end up getting divorced, or we resign as missionaries and stay married." What happened next was only because of God!

WE NEVER GIVE UP

I've always said that man was designed for accomplishment, engineered for success, and endowed with the seeds of greatness...Every person has unique gifts, and those gifts give him or her the power and the opportunity to accomplish great things, if he or she learns how to use those gifts and channel them in the right direction.[39]

One day Elisha the prophet went to the town of Shunem. A wealthy woman lived there, and she urged him to come to her home for a meal. After that, whenever he passed that way, he would stop there for something to eat (2 Kings 4:8).

Stepping back into the Old Testament, we discover a woman who was determined to meet the needs of God's servant Elisha whenever he was in the neighborhood. She had no obligation to do so. If anything, it was the generosity in her heart that drove her to bless Elisha in this way. Naturally, I can only think that Elisha was grateful for her help. Imagine if you had chosen to follow Jehovah God with no guarantee of a salary—actually no guarantee of any kind. I'm sure there would be days of abundant blessing, but also days of loneliness, solitude, or even discouragement, knowing that what you thought God would do was different from what He actually did. Elisha may have thought to himself, *This lady is incredible. Wouldn't it be awesome if I could somehow bless her?* Elisha asked his servant Gehazi how he thought they could bless her, and the following conversation took place:

"She doesn't have a son, and her husband is an old man."

"Call her back again," Elisha told him. When the woman returned, Elisha said to her as she stood in the doorway, "Next year at this time you will be holding a son in your arms!"

"No, my lord!" she cried. "O man of God, don't deceive me and get my hopes up like that."

But sure enough, the woman soon became pregnant. And at that time the following year she had a son (2 Kings 4:14-17).

Now, if I were this lady, I'd say that God's miracle was spot on! Not having children or being able to bear children in this area of the world was humiliating. As an example, Genesis 30 tells us that Rachel, when struggling to get pregnant, became so jealous she said she would die if Jacob couldn't give her children of her own (v. 1). In the International Standard Bible Encyclopedia, we read that "In Israel and among oriental peoples generally barrenness was a woman's and a family's greatest misfortune."[40] This story in no way, shape, or form appears in the Bible by chance. God is saying something here. While no one knows why God chose to do this miracle, a possible reason is that He was interested in her and her future. He knew certain needs in this woman's life could only be met by an immediate miracle and a future pain. God also knew that this woman couldn't understand His reasoning for future pain, but it was necessary. In fact, it saved her life. Yes, a future intense pain proved to save her life. What was this future pain that God kept under wraps when He performed that miracle baby?

The child grew, and one day he went out to his father, who was with the reapers. He said to his father, "My head! My head!" His father told a servant, "Carry him to his mother." After the servant had lifted him up and carried him to his mother, the boy sat on her lap until noon, and then he died (2 Kings 4:18-20).

The woman told Elisha, "Please, man of God, don't mislead your servant!" (v. 16). I can imagine her throwing herself at Elisha's feet, begging him to intervene, and begging him to seek God for a second miracle. Even she realized that such a miracle was beyond impossible; it was absurd. She had not asked for the child. All she had wanted to do was help the man of God, and as a result, he blessed her with a child. He saw her shame of barrenness and had great mercy. How was it then that God could allow this child to die? How could such a caring, loving God build someone's hopes so high only to crush them in extreme devastation?

And Michele will tell you, when she was separated from our ministry in Costa Rica, it was as though someone died. While she hadn't initially intended to work in this area of ministry, God had aligned the pieces so perfectly for us to make a difference in Costa Rica. And now? It felt as though death came knocking at the door, and it ravaged our home. It almost cost us our marriage. Not only did that death affect us, but it also affected our kids. Isabella had to see her mom go through such a difficult time that she one time declared, "I want my mom back!" All three of us had to go to counseling. It made no sense that we had to go to counseling simply for serving God. Just like that Shunamite woman, we questioned God and His goodness.

It might seem natural to stop at this point in the woman's story or as well as the Pérez family story and say, "It's over." But God wasn't finished. Keep following the storyline; you eventually get to the unexpected, supernatural wisdom of God in the most powerful four words of chapter 8, verse 5. Those words were "at that very moment." I love that wording. "At that very moment." All of the pain, all of the hardship, all of the suffering —suddenly, it all made sense. If you think God was being cruel, you run the risk of missing the miracle that's only made available through pain.

Elisha came and prayed for this boy to come back to life in

response to the woman's plea. After seven attempts of stretching himself upon the boy, the writer tells us the boy sneezed seven times and opened his eyes (2 Kings 4:35). The story sounds too strange to be true, but that's God. As I've said, God will not allow himself to be put in a box nor confined to human-constructed methodologies. It was important for Elisha to know that he wasn't the healer. At the same time, Elisha and the woman both needed to recognize God as the healer because this miracle was about more than the prophet and the mother. This miracle was about God and about what He and He alone is capable of doing.

Her son died, and he was resurrected, and then the prophet told her to leave her land and home for the next seven years. There would be a famine, and the only way to survive was to leave. There's no explanation as to why the boy died. I don't read of any explanation being given to her either. The only thing she appears to hear is, "Lady, here's your boy, now go, for seven years."

That often mirrors our experience with God. We don't get an explanation; He gives us no clue as to why we had to experience a triumph, a pain, a victory, or a defeat. I still had no clue why things fell apart so quickly with our partner organization in Costa Rica. God continued to treat me with what I considered radio silence. That didn't mean God was absent, nor did it mean He was uninterested. It meant the only two things we could do were to obey his instructions and follow after Him. That's all He asks. God never promised to give us an explanation. Look at the disciples when Jesus went to the cross and died. They never in their wildest dreams expected that Jesus would die, but He did. He had to. And those disciples would have to be content with obeying and following.

Finally, at the end of seven years, the woman came back home. She walked into the king's chambers when, "at that very moment," Gehazi was there telling her story to the king (2 Kings

8:5). You can call it coincidence, or you can trust in the processes of God that will always put us at the right place and time if we're willing to obey his instructions and follow after him. For God's plan to achieve its purpose in this woman's life, her son had to die. It was necessary! Whether she understood it or not, it was necessary. She allowed herself to submit to the process, to the prophet's command, even though God had caused her incredible pain and many tears. Then the king spoke to his officials, directly commanding them to restore to her "everything she had lost...including the value of any crops that had been harvested during her absence" (2 Kings 8:6). She didn't understand anything that happened until right at that very moment. Perhaps she broke out again in tears, thanking God with a heart of pure gratitude. "God, thank you that my son died. Thank you for his resurrection. Thank you for the famine. Thank you for keeping me alive. Now, because of you, because of my needed pain, life will be beyond my wildest expectations." Only God.

On June 8, 2019, I was invited to a lunch where God spoke for the second time since that dreadful day in the boardroom. We honestly thought we had reached the end of the road. At that time, Michele and I were about to resign as missionaries. We enjoyed a fun conversation and some great Mexican food during our lunch hour, all until we had an "at that very moment" experience. For the first time in over a year, we understood exactly why we had to go through such a dreadful season of pain. This pain required us to recognize that we had to be prepared to stop because there would be delays ahead. At that lunch, some friends mentioned that our names were brought up at a prayer meeting in Havana, Cuba, in December of the previous year. To think that God would do something like that was breathtaking. A committed group of people had started to pray for us over the next few months until that lunch meeting. Friends that I thought were calling out of concern during our marriage struggles revealed that they were really calling because they needed to gauge where we were in our restoration process. To top it all off, my old regional director, who had told me many years earlier never to mention Cuba, was sitting at the table with his wife. I was so confused. I wondered, *What is God doing? What in the world is happening?*

Then the "at that very moment" experience took place. The area director for Cuba said, "Bob, Michele, we've been looking to recruit a new, young couple for Cuba for some time now. Now we can't recruit just any candidate. First, this couple should be able to speak Spanish; second, they have to know Cuban culture; and third, this couple must have been through hell in ministry and have something of value to offer the Cuban people."

And then I heard the voice of the Lord jump in my spirit. The area director said, "We'd love to invite you to come and work with us in Cuba." We couldn't believe our ears. Were we hearing him right? After everything that had happened in our lives, now this? Was God really opening the doors for ministry in Cuba? I was overwhelmed beyond words. Like the Shunamite woman, we understood for the very first time. Similar to how her child had died, our ministry had died, and it was now being resurrected back to life. God was giving us a second chance. Or should I say, He had finally positioned us to respond to that call I received when I was a kid in the church in Blackwood. I wasn't crazy. Everything was one hundred percent part of God's plan all along; I just didn't know because I didn't need to know. But that day, it was clear, God was speaking without speaking, and He said, "I'm not done with you yet." Trust me; I had wanted to give up and call it quits—many times. We were surviving by a thread and the fact that we hung on, despite thinking that God had somehow abandoned us. These people saw our grittiness and willingness to hang on. They invited us to serve the area and country that I had requested fifteen years before because of a calling I received as a boy some thirty years earlier.

One Final Challenge for You as a Reader

If you have decided to follow Jesus Christ, if you're staying close to the Master, if you're seeking wise counsel and spending time with God, and it still feels you're in the dark, don't give up. Maybe you're even going through hell and are considering giving up on God, your call, and His plan, don't. This is not the time to surrender. If you follow God, there will be delays, but there will also be moments when you must push ahead. I guarantee you; there will be days when you must be prepared to stop, but we must never give up on seeking to hear from God.

Listen to the Apostle Paul, the author of nearly the entire New Testament of our Bible:

> We are pressed on every side by troubles, but we are not crushed. We are perplexed, but not driven to despair. [9] We are hunted down, but never abandoned by God. We get knocked down, but we are not destroyed. [10] Through suffering, our bodies continue to share in the death of Jesus so that the life of Jesus may also be seen in our bodies...[13] But we continue to preach because we have the same kind of faith the psalmist had when he said, "I believed in God, so I spoke."
>
> ...And as God's grace reaches more and more people, there will be great thanksgiving, and God will receive more and more glory. That is why we never give up (2 Corinthians 4:8-13, 15 NLT).

David Platt[41] wrote, "The question for us, then, is whether we trust in His power. And the problem for us is that in our culture we are tempted at every turn to trust in our own power instead. So the challenge for us is to live in such a way that we are radically dependent on and desperate for the power that only God can provide." By God's design, as followers of Christ, we are expected to walk out our faith in a way that demonstrates a difference from the world around us.

There are monumental decisions that we will need to make along the way. Unfortunately, not every decision will have an answer clearly marked out in Scripture, but you can trust Psalm 25:12, "Who are those who fear the Lord? He will show them the path they should follow." Maybe there is never an audible voice. Maybe there is no big spectacle or some grand outward sign that will mark the path we should follow. Maybe the path God designed for us can only be known by learning sensitivity to that internal voice that comes only from God.

Missions has been my life for nearly two decades. The story God has written for us has been an incredible journey. I can honestly say I believe I have heard the Lord, and I have followed. I do not always get it right, but there is no question that I am "radically dependent on and desperate for the power that only God can provide."[42] But that is my story.

He is also writing a new story with you. He wants to change the world, your family, your circle of influence because of your life—your story. I pray that the stories on the pages of this book ignite a fire in you that will encourage you to listen for God's voice. I am sure that if you still yourself long enough, if you'll sit with Him long enough, if you'll get his life manual (the Bible) inside of you, when God says its time, you'll be able to say, "God spoke, and I heard!"

ABOUT THE AUTHOR

Roberto (Bob) began his missionary career in 2004. During his first missionary term in Santiago, Chile, Roberto served as an itinerate evangelist. He was a member of the Chilean National Church Planting Committee.

In 2010, Roberto and his wife transferred to Costa Rica. There, he was elected the Presbyter of the Atlantic Coast. He led transformation efforts in a section of the country that has been stagnant for nearly twenty-five years. Roberto was the national church health director responsible for the development of a nationwide church health initiative. He and Michele worked together with a local NGO engaged in addressing the crimes of human trafficking. Together with this partner organization, they collaborated to build a safehouse restoration facility, participated in search and rescue operations, led targeted discipleship efforts, and so much more.

In 2020, they began their work on the island nation of Cuba.

Bob graduated from the Assemblies of God Global University with his Bachelors in Intercultural Studies. He received his MBA from Bellevue University in 2014. In 2018, he graduated with his doctorate in Business Administration and a specialization in Public Administration. His thesis work addressed the impact Costa Rican female legislators have on legislative outcomes related to addressing the issue of human trafficking.

NOTES

[1]

Ruth Haley Barton, *Sacred Rhythms : Arranging Our Lives for Spiritual Transformation* (Downers Grove, Ill., InterVarsity Press, 2006), 12.

[2] Lou Engle, *The Fast: Rediscovering Jesus' Pathway to Power* (Colorado Springs, CO: Engle House Publishing, 2020), 7.

[3] https://www.youtube.com/watch?v=2dCvSafgCgw

[4] https://www.youtube.com/watch?v=GRjiOVsUF6o

[5] Stan E. DeKoven, *Fresh Manna: Introduction to the Study of God's Word* (Ramona, CA: Vision Publishing, 1990), 7. http://library.melbac.org/books/vision/Fresh%20Manna.pdf

[6]   https://www.christianity.com/jesus/birth-of-jesus/genealogy-and-jewish-heritage/rahab-harlot-liar-ancestor-of-jesus.html

[7] https://www.sbc.net/about/what-we-do/faq/

[8] https://www.focusonthefamily.ca/content/parenting-your-teen-as-they-wrestle-with-their-faith

[9] Pat Williams and James Denney, *Character Carved in Stone* (Grand Rapids, MI: Revell), 46.

[10] Ed Stetzer and Mike Dodson, *Comeback Churches* (Nashville, TN: B & H Publishing House, 2007) 107-108.

[11] Alicia Britt Nicole, *40 Days of Decrease* (Nashville, TN: W Publishing Goup, 2016), 10. W Publishing Group.

[12] Pat Williams and James Denney, *Character Carved in Stone* (Grand Rapids, MI: Revell), 66.

[13]   https://ag.org/-/media/AGORG/Beliefs/Position-Papers/PP_The_Kingdom_of_God.pdf

[14]   https://churchleaders.com/pastors/pastor-articles/162723-how-god-works-through-desert-experiences.html

[15] Max Lucado, *Facing Your Giants: God Still Does the Impossible* (Nashville, TN: Thomas Nelson, 2006), 26.

[16] Ruth Haley Barton, *Sacred Rhythms: Arranging Our Lives for Spiritual Transformation* (Downers Grove, Ill., InterVarsity Press, 2006), 110

[17] Ruth Haley Barton, *Sacred Rhythms: Arranging Our Lives for Spiritual Transformation* (Downers Grove, Ill., InterVarsity Press, 2006), 27.

[18] Jeff Hartensveld, *Apostolic Spark: Igniting the Church for the Final Harvest* (Springfield, MO: Assemblies of God World Missions), Kindle Edition.

[19] Speed the Light (STL) - Speed the Light is a branch of the Assemblies of God

Youth Department that works with the youth to purchase vehicles and other evangelistic equipping material for our Assemblies of God on the ground missionaries.

[20] Kent Ingle, *Framework leadership: Position yourself for transformational change* (Springfield, MO: Salubris Resources, 2017), Location No. 142.

[21] https://jdgreear.com/four-ways-gods-spirit-speaks-to-our-spirit-part-1/

[22] John Piper and David Mathis, Thinking. Loving. Doing. (Contributions by: R. Albert Mohler Jr., R. C. Sproul, Rick Warren, Francis Chan, John Piper, Thabiti Anyabwile): A Call to Glorify God with Heart and Mind (Kindle Location 609). Crossway. Kindle Edition.

[23] Thomas E. Trask, Wayde I. Goodall, and Zenas J. Bicket, (Springfield, MO: Gospel Publishing House, 1997), 29-30.

[24] Doris Kearns Goodwin, *Leadership in Turbulent Times* (New York: Simon and Schuster, 2010), 14.

[25] https://www.homeaffairs.gov.au/criminal-justice/files/nap-combat-modern-slavery-2020-25.pdf

[26] https://www.ministrystudiesonline.com

[27] https://www.desiringgod.org/articles/god-will-sustain-you-a-day-at-a-time

[28] Stanley Horton, *Genesis: The Promise of Blessing* (Springfield, MO: World Library Press,1996), 165.

[29] Max Lucado, *Facing Your Giants: God Still Does the Impossible* (Nashville, TN: Thomas Nelson, 2006), 88.

[30] https://biblehub.com/commentaries/jfb/matthew/7.htm

[31] Peter Scazzero, *The Emotionally Healthy Leader: How Transforming Your Inner Life Will Deeply Transform Your Church, Team, and the World* (Grand Rapids, MI: Zondervan, 2015), Kindle Locations 4992-4994.

[32] Timothy Ferriss, *Tribe of Mentors* (New York: Houghton Mifflin Harcourt Publishing Company, 2017), 32.

[33] Peter Scazzero, *The Emotionally Healthy Leader: How Transforming Your Inner Life Will Deeply Transform Your Church, Team, and the World* (Grand Rapids, MI: Zondervan, 2015), 285.

[34] https://www.barna.com/research/covid-19-pastor-emotions/

[35] https://enrichmentjournal.ag.org/Issues/2009/Spring-2009/When-Sheep-Attack

[36] Peter Scazzero, *The Emotionally Healthy Leader: How Transforming Your Inner Life Will Deeply Transform Your Church, Team, and the World* (Grand Rapids, MI: Zondervan, 2015), Kindle Locations 4992-4994.

[37] Terrence Real. The New Rules of Marriage (p. 5). Random House Publishing Group. Kindle Edition.

[38] Terrence Real. The New Rules of Marriage (p. 5). Random House Publishing Group. Kindle Edition.

[39] Zig Ziglar and Tom Ziglar, *Born to Win: Find Your Success Code* (Made for Success Publishing, 2014), Location No. 293.

[40]   https://www.studylight.org/encyclopedias/eng/isb/b/barren-barrenness.html

[41] David Platt, *Radical: Taking Back your Faith from the American Dream* (New York: Multnomah, 2010). 45.

[42] David Platt, *Radical: Taking Back your Faith from the American Dream* (New York: Multnomah, 2010). 45.

Made in the USA
Columbia, SC
13 July 2021